Taxcafe Tax Guides

Pension Magic

How to Make the Taxman
Pay for Your Retirement

By Nick Braun PhD

Important Legal Notices:

Published by:
Taxcafe UK Limited
67 Milton Road
Kirkcaldy KY1 1TL
Tel: (0044) 01592 560081
Email: team@taxcafe.co.uk

Third Edition, April 2014

ISBN 978-1-907302-83-1

Trademarks
Taxcafe® is a registered trademark of Taxcafe UK Limited. All other trademarks, names and logos in this tax guide may be trademarks of their respective owners.

Disclaimer
Before reading or relying on the content of this tax guide please read the disclaimer.

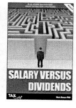

Disclaimer

1. This guide is intended as **general guidance** only and does NOT constitute accountancy, tax, financial, investment or other professional advice.

2. The author and Taxcafe UK Limited make no representations or warranties with respect to the accuracy or completeness of this publication and cannot accept any responsibility or liability for any loss or risk, personal or otherwise, which may arise, directly or indirectly, from reliance on information contained in this publication.

3. Please note that tax legislation, the law and practices by Government and regulatory authorities (e.g. HM Revenue & Customs) are constantly changing. We therefore recommend that for accountancy, tax, financial, investment or other professional advice, you consult a suitably qualified accountant, tax advisor, financial adviser, or other professional adviser.

4. Please also note that your personal circumstances may vary from the general examples given in this guide and your professional adviser will be able to give specific advice based on your personal circumstances.

5. This guide covers UK taxation only and any references to 'tax' or 'taxation', unless the contrary is expressly stated, refer to UK taxation only. Please note that references to the 'UK' do not include the Channel Islands or the Isle of Man. Foreign tax implications are beyond the scope of this guide.

6. All persons described in the examples in this guide are entirely fictional. Any similarities to actual persons, living or dead, or to fictional characters created by any other author, are entirely coincidental.

Dedication

Once again, to Aileen for all your love and support and to Jake, Sandy and Tilly for all the joy you bring.

About the Author & Taxcafe

Dr Nick Braun founded Taxcafe in 1999, along with his partner Aileen Smith. As the driving force behind the company, their aim is to provide affordable plain-English tax information for private individuals, business owners and professional advisors.

Over the past 14 years Taxcafe has become one of the best-known tax publishers in the UK and has won several prestigious business awards.

Nick has been a specialist tax writer since 1989, first in South Africa, where he edited the monthly *Tax Breaks* publication, and since 1999 in the UK, where he has authored several tax books including *Property Capital Gains Tax*, and *Small Business Tax Saving Tactics*.

Nick also has a PhD in economics from the University of Glasgow, where he was awarded the prestigious William Glen scholarship and later became a Research Fellow.

Contents

Introduction

Let's get straight down to business. There is only one reason why you should put money into a pension and that is to SAVE TAX.

When you put money into a pension you enjoy two important tax reliefs:

- Tax relief on your contributions – what I call buying investments at a 40% discount.

- Tax-free growth – all your income and capital gains are completely tax free.

However, if *maximising* tax relief is your priority, as it should be, there's a lot more to it than simply putting away a fixed amount each year.

You may want to decide *how much* to invest, making bigger or smaller pension contributions in some tax years, or none at all.

You may want to consider *who* makes the contributions (you, your employer, or your spouse).

You may also want to look at *when* is the best time to invest.

And, of course, you may want to know *why* you should even bother investing in a pension in the first place. For example, are pensions better than other investments, like ISAs?

All of these important issues are addressed in this guide and I think you will be surprised by some of the results.

In Part 1 we explain how tax relief on pension contributions is calculated and the rules that determine how much you are allowed to invest.

However, calculating the maximum pension contribution you *can* make is not really the important issue. What is far more important, and fully explained in this part of the guide, is calculating the maximum pension contribution you *should* make to get extra tax relief.

Over 400,000 people do not claim all the tax relief to which they are entitled, so we also explain how you can make backdated claims and avoid other common mistakes that could cost you thousands of pounds.

Pension Freedom is Coming

Right now the amount of money you can withdraw from your pension is tightly controlled. Most individuals' savings can only come out at a trickle, either through one of those universally detested annuities or something not much better called "capped drawdown".

However, this restriction will soon be lifted following George Osborne's announcement in the March 2014 Budget that:

"We will legislate to remove all remaining tax restrictions on how pensioners have access to their pension pots. Pensioners will have complete freedom to draw down as much or as little of their pension pot as they want, anytime they want. No caps. No drawdown limits. Let me be clear. No one will have to buy an annuity."

These changes are revolutionary and will result in pension savers having more control over their money than they have ever had.

At the stroke of a pen the Government has removed one of the biggest obstacles that deters people from using pensions to save for retirement.

The new withdrawal rules will only apply from April 2015 and the Government is currently consulting on the changes. However, the existing restrictions are largely academic if you are several years away from retirement.

For the first time, pension savers will have the freedom to control their tax bills, by making big pension withdrawals in some tax years and smaller withdrawals in others.

In Part 2 of the guide we explain, using lots of detailed examples, how you will be able to save thousands of pounds in both income tax and capital gains tax by timing your pension withdrawals carefully.

Pensions versus ISAs

In Part 3 we show how pensions are much more powerful tax shelters than ISAs. We track two investors over a number of years and reveal that a pension saver could end up with as much as 71% more retirement income than an ISA investor.

We also explain some of the lesser known tax differences between ISAs and pensions (for example, why some dividend income is taxed inside an ISA and why your family may be better off if your money is in a pension).

In Part 4 we look at the pros and cons of postponing and accelerating pension contributions. We show how basic-rate taxpayers (those earning under £41,865 in 2014/15) can increase their pension pots by 33% by delaying making pension contributions for several years.

This part of the guide also contains a fascinating case study which reveals that – even if you postpone making pension contributions for several years – you will not end up one penny worse off than someone who makes pension contributions for many years.

There is one group who should always consider making pension contributions: households where the highest earner's income is between £50,000 and £60,000 and child benefit is being claimed.

Your family's child benefit payments are steadily taken away as income rises from £50,000 to £60,000. As a result, by using pension contributions to reduce taxable income, people in this income bracket will enjoy tax relief of up to 72% or more! Full details in Part 4.

Employees, Business Owners & Landlords

In Parts 5 to 8 we look at different types of pension saver: regular salaried employees, company directors, self-employed business owners and landlords.

In Part 5 we explain 'auto-enrolment': the new system of compulsory pensions that will see many employees enjoy a pension contribution from their employers for the first time.

Many individuals who can receive free money from their employers in the shape of a company pension contribution do not take up the offer. So in this part of the guide we also publish an interesting table that shows you just how much bigger your pension pot will be if you take full advantage of the free cash your employer is offering.

Part 6 looks at salary sacrifice pensions, which can boost your pension pot by an astonishing 34%! Salary sacrifice pensions allow you to claw back not just income tax but *national insurance* as well, including the 13.8% national insurance paid by your employer.

A salary sacrifice pension is not just a tax-efficient way to save for retirement, it is arguably the most powerful tax-saving tool available to salaried employees.

Part 7 covers company owners and directors and reveals how they can enjoy 42.5% tax relief on their own pension contributions (most higher-rate taxpayers only receive 40%). We also look at how getting your company to make pension contributions on your behalf is a highly tax-efficient way to extract additional money from the business.

Most of this guide is relevant to self-employed business owners (sole traders and the like). However, some additional practical pointers are provided in Part 8 to help this group maximise their tax relief.

I've also included a chapter here for landlords. It explains how, with the help of a pension, you can avoid paying income tax on your rental income, thereby giving your property investments extra fire power.

Finally, we get to Part 9 which, with the help of a detailed case study, answers a key family pension planning question: "Who should make the pension contributions, me or my spouse/partner?"

And in the last chapter we look at the pros and cons of opening a pension for your children or grandchildren.

I hope you find it an enjoyable and interesting read.

Scope of this Guide

This guide does not cover every aspect of pension saving. The focus is *maximising tax relief*, which is the main reason people invest in the first place.

I do not cover issues like pension charges, how you should invest your money (in shares, bonds, property etc), or how to choose a pension provider.

I make no excuses for these omissions. As it is, I've struggled to keep the guide to around 200 pages, focusing almost entirely on tax saving strategies. Other pension issues are all covered very well by others in the financial media.

Furthermore, all of the coverage in this guide is about defined contribution pension schemes, also known as money purchase schemes. These include personal pensions, SIPPs, and their corporate equivalents. The basic idea is you (and maybe your employer) put money in, and what level of pension you get out at the end of the day, depends on how well the investments perform.

All individual pensions are structured along these lines and most corporate pension schemes are moving in this direction, if they haven't done so already.

There is no discussion of defined benefit or final salary pension schemes. In January 2012, Royal Dutch Shell announced plans to close its final salary scheme to new entrants. This marked the end of an era because Shell was the last remaining FTSE 100 company to offer this type of pension scheme.

For many company employees, final salary schemes are now a thing of the past. If you belong to one, all I can say is, I'm jealous!

Finally, please remember that this guide is not meant to be a substitute for proper professional advice. Before you act you should contact either a suitably qualified accountant, tax advisor, IFA or pensions expert who understands your personal circumstances.

Part 1

Putting Money In:
The Pension Contribution Rules

Chapter 1

Tax Relief on Contributions: How it's Calculated

When you make pension contributions the taxman will top up your savings by paying cash directly into your plan. Effectively for every £80 you invest, the taxman will put in an extra £20.

Why £20, you might be asking? Well your contributions are treated as having been paid out of income that has already been taxed at the basic income tax rate of 20%. The taxman is therefore refunding the income tax you've already paid.

The company that manages your pension plan – usually an insurance company or SIPP provider – will claim this money for you from the taxman and credit it to your account.

So whatever contribution you make personally, divide it by 0.80 and you'll get the total amount that is invested in your pension pot.

Example
Peter invests £4,000 in a self-invested personal pension (SIPP). After the taxman makes his top-up payment, the total amount of money Peter will have sitting in his pension pot is £5,000:

$$£4,000/0.80 = £5,000$$

Basic-rate tax relief isn't the end of the story. If Peter is a *higher-rate* taxpayer, paying tax at 40%, he'll be able to claim even more tax relief.

The Cherry on Top – Higher Rate Relief

For the 2014/15 tax year a higher-rate taxpayer is generally someone who earns more than £41,865.

If you are a higher-rate taxpayer the taxman will let you claim your higher-rate tax relief when you submit your tax return.

Alternatively, if you are a company employee, higher-rate tax relief can be provided immediately by reducing the tax paid on your salary via your PAYE code.

(See Chapter 4 for more information on how to claim higher-rate tax relief.)

Example
As we already know, Peter's personal contribution is £4,000 and total pension fund investment, including the taxman's top-up, is:

$$£4,000/0.80 = £5,000$$

The £4,000 is what's known as the 'net contribution' and the £5,000 is what's known as the 'gross contribution'.

Multiplying the gross contribution by 20% (40% – 20%) we get:

$$£5,000 \times 20\% = £1,000$$

This is Peter's higher-rate tax relief.

Effectively he has a pension investment of £5,000 which has cost him just £3,000 (£4,000 personal contribution less his £1,000 tax refund). In other words, he is getting all of his investments at a 40% discount.

This is the critical number. Being able to make investments year after year at a 40% discount can have a huge effect on the amount of wealth you accumulate.

Summary

- When you make pension contributions you qualify for two types of tax relief: Basic-rate tax relief which comes in the shape of top-ups to your pension plan and higher-rate relief which is normally claimed when you submit your tax return.

- Your total pension fund investment is found by dividing your personal contribution by 0.80. The taxman's top-up is paid directly to your pension provider who will credit your pension pot.

- Higher-rate relief is calculated by multiplying your gross pension fund contribution by 20%.

- Together these two tax reliefs mean all your pension investments come in at a 40% discount.

Chapter 2

How Much Can You Invest?

In this chapter we will examine the rules that determine how much you can invest in a pension each year.

Note that successive governments have continually tampered with the pension system, for better or worse. If you are making pension contributions over several decades you should not rely on the same set of rules applying in 5, 10 or 20 years' time.

The good news, for now at least, is that it's possible to make quite big pension contributions and enjoy full income tax relief.

Age

This is a good one to kick off with. Generally anyone up to the ripe old age of 75 can make pension contributions.

In the future it may even be possible to make contributions if you are 75 or older. In the March 2014 Budget the Government announced that it will explore whether this age limit should be changed or abolished.

There is effectively no lower age limit. You may not be able to set up your own pension plan if you are under 18 years of age but some pension providers have special products so that parents and grandparents can make pension contributions for their children and grandchildren (see Chapter 35 for more information).

Multiple Pension Schemes

Up until a few years ago many members of workplace schemes could not contribute to a second pension, such as a self-invested personal pension (SIPP). This is no longer the case.

Most people can now contribute to more than one pension plan and have more control over how their retirement savings are invested.

The Basic Pension Contribution Rule

To obtain tax relief on your pension contributions they have to stay within certain limits:

- **Earnings.** Contributions made by you *personally* must not exceed your annual earnings.

- **The £40,000 Annual Allowance.** Total pension contributions by you and anyone else (normally your employer) must not exceed £40,000 per year. The annual allowance was reduced from £50,000 to £40,000 at the start of the 2014/15 tax year.

Ignoring any pension contributions by an employer, an individual with earnings of £35,000 can contribute £35,000 to a pension. An individual with earnings of £75,000 can contribute £40,000 (contributions capped by the annual allowance).

If there are employer contributions as well, these also have to be thrown into the pot when calculating the maximum pension contribution.

Let's say the individual with earnings of £75,000 is an employee and his employer contributes £10,000 to his pension. The maximum contribution he can make personally is £30,000:

£40,000 annual allowance – £10,000 from employer = £30,000

How Relevant Is this to Me?

Almost everyone making pension contributions needs to understand what is meant by the term 'earnings'. Earnings are not the same as income.

The annual allowance, on the other hand, is completely irrelevant to the vast majority of people because very few of us have anything close to £40,000 paid into our pension plans each year.

However, as we shall see in Part 4, there may be times when you want to make big catch-up contributions. In these circumstances it is important to know a bit more about how the annual allowance operates.

Gross vs Cash Contributions

The above pension contribution limits are for *gross* pension contributions. However, the money you actually pay into your pension is normally NOT a gross pension contribution (unless you belong to certain types of occupational pension scheme). To calculate your gross contributions you have to add on basic-rate tax relief (the taxman's top up). You do that by dividing your actual cash contribution by 0.80.

How does this affect the pension contribution limits? If you have earnings of £35,000 you cannot pay £35,000 into your pension plan. You can only pay in £28,000 (£35,000 x 0.8). The taxman will add a further £7,000 in tax relief, bringing your total gross pension contribution to £35,000.

Similarly, the £40,000 annual allowance is a cap on total gross pension contributions. So the maximum cash pension contribution an individual can make in the absence of any employer contributions, is £32,000 (£40,000 x 0.8), with the taxman adding a further £8,000 in tax relief.

Employer Contributions

Contributions by employers are always gross contributions. When your employer puts money into your pension plan there is no additional top up from the taxman. (Instead the company obtains tax relief by claiming employee pension contributions as a tax deductible business expense.)

So if your employer contributes £10,000 to your pension that will be a gross contribution and the maximum gross contribution you can make personally is £30,000:

£40,000 – £10,000 = £30,000

The maximum amount you can actually pay into your pension plan would then be £24,000:

£30,000 x 0.8 = £24,000

You can only make this maximum contribution if you have earnings of at least £30,000.

Occupational Pension Schemes

For many employees who belong to occupational schemes, the actual pension contribution is the same as the gross pension contribution.

Under the popular 'net pay arrangement' the employer often deducts the employee's pension contributions from the employee's gross pay before tax is deducted.

This means full tax relief is obtained immediately by paying the contribution out of pre-tax income. There is no top up by the taxman and no need to claim any higher-rate tax relief via a tax return.

Not all contributions by employees are made gross. If the employer has a pension scheme that uses 'relief at source' (usually group personal pensions), the employee's contributions are paid into the pension scheme after the employee's salary has been taxed. Basic-rate relief is then claimed by the pension scheme and added to the member's pension pot to obtain their total gross pension contribution.

Earnings

To obtain tax relief on your pension contributions you have to have earnings – 'relevant UK earnings' to be precise.

Employees

If you are an employee, your relevant UK earnings will include:

- Salary or wages
- Bonus, overtime, and commissions, and
- Taxable benefits in kind.

There are a few other bits and bobs that can count as relevant UK earnings for pension contribution purposes, including redundancy payments that exceed the £30,000 tax-free threshold and statutory sick pay and statutory maternity pay.

Company Directors

Most small company owners are also directors. For pension contribution purposes company directors are treated just like regular employees. Their relevant UK earnings include their salary, bonus, overtime, commissions and taxable benefits in kind.

As shareholders of their companies they can also pay themselves dividends. To save tax and national insurance, many company owners take a small tax-free salary and take the rest of their income as dividends.

For owners of small companies it is generally tax efficient to pay yourself a salary equal to the national insurance threshold (£7,956 for 2014/15) and take the rest of your income as dividends. (See Chapter 30.)

The problem, however, is that dividends are NOT earnings. As such, a company director with a salary of £7,956 and dividends of £50,000 can only contribute £7,956 to a pension.

The actual cash contribution would be £6,365 (£7,956 x 0.8) with the taxman adding £1,591 in tax relief for a gross contribution of £7,956.

Fortunately for company owners, they can also get their companies to make additional pension contributions (employer contributions) and these are not restricted to their earnings (although they are restricted by the £40,000 annual allowance). We'll take a closer look at pension planning for company directors in Part 7.

The Self-Employed

Most people would regard any business owner as 'self-employed'. However, when HMRC talks about 'self-employed' individuals they are referring specifically to owners of unincorporated businesses, in other words businesses that are not companies.

The most common are sole traders (one-person businesses) and partnerships.

If you are a sole trader your relevant UK earnings are generally the pre-tax profits of the business. If you are a partner, your relevant UK earnings will be your share of the partnership's pre-tax profit.

The problem is that many self-employed individuals don't know what their pre-tax profits are!

Many have an accounting period that is the same as the tax year, running to 5 April each year or 31 March. This can create a practical problem when it comes to maximising tax relief on pension contributions.

Although most salary earners (including company directors) have earnings that are fairly predictable (their salaries), the exact profits on which self-employed business owners can base their pension contributions may not be known until the accounts are drawn up *after* the tax year has ended.

In other words, as a self-employed business owner you may only know what your relevant UK earnings are when it is too late to make pension contributions. You cannot make back-dated pension contributions after the tax year has ended. I'll explain how this practical problem can be fixed in Chapter 32.

Income but Not Earnings

Earnings do not include:

- Rental income
- Interest
- Dividends
- Capital gains

For example, if you have earnings of £30,000 and rental income of £20,000 from buy-to-let properties, the maximum gross pension contribution you can make is £30,000.

With regards to rental income, there is one exception. When it comes to tax, owners of furnished holiday lettings are treated quite differently to other rental property owners and pensions are no exception. Profits from furnished holiday lettings count as relevant UK earnings for pension purposes.

Individuals with No Earnings

Some people don't have any earnings, including non-working spouses and minor children.

Many professional landlords, who derive all of their income from rental properties, will also not have any earnings.

The good news is that everyone under the age of 75 can make a pension contribution of £3,600 per year, regardless of earnings.

The actual cash contribution would be £2,880, with the taxman adding £720 to bring the total gross contribution to £3,600.

We'll take a closer look at the pros and cons of making pension contributions when you have no earnings in Part 9.

The Annual Allowance

The annual allowance is the overall cap on pension contributions that enjoy tax relief.

For 2014/15 and future tax years the annual allowance is £40,000 (previously £50,000).

The annual allowance includes pension contributions made by both you and anyone else (normally your employer). In other words, the contributions you make and the contributions anyone else makes should not exceed the annual allowance.

Even if contributions to your pension plans do exceed the annual allowance, you can carry forward unused allowance from earlier tax years (see below).

If the annual allowance is exceeded, and the excess is not covered by carry forward, you will have to pay tax on the excess at your marginal income tax rate (20%, 40% or 45%). This annual allowance charge can be paid when you submit your tax return or deducted from your pension savings if it is over £2,000.

In practice, the contribution limits are quite generous and very few people will be affected by them. Those who have to be most careful are those making big one-off pension contributions.

Another group that has to be careful are members of final salary or defined benefit pension schemes. The value of their pension benefits can increase by significantly more than £40,000 in the year they receive a substantial pay increase. Professional advice should also be obtained in these circumstances.

The Carry Forward Rule

If you want to make a big pension contribution of over £40,000 in 2014/15, you can tap any unused allowance from the three previous tax years. This means you can potentially make a pension contribution of up to £190,000 and enjoy full tax relief (£40,000 for the current tax year and £50,000 for each of the previous three tax years – because the annual allowance was £50,000 in those tax years).

Example

Paula is a sole trader and makes bumper profits of £150,000 during the 2014/15 tax year. She transfers £80,000 into her pension plan, resulting in a gross pension contribution of £100,000 (£80,000/0.8). Her gross pension contributions in the three previous tax years were:

	Pension Contribution	Unused Annual Allowance
2013/14	£20,000	£30,000
2012/13	£30,000	£20,000
2011/12	£30,000	£20,000

In total Paula has £70,000 of unused annual allowance. Together with the £40,000 annual allowance for the current tax year, Paula can make a total gross pension contribution of up to £110,000. Her £100,000 gross pension contribution is therefore within the limits and does not exceed her earnings and therefore enjoys full tax relief.

You use the annual allowance for the current tax year first. You then use your unused annual allowance from the *earliest* tax year first (2011/12 in Paula's case).

This leaves any unused allowance from the most recent tax years free to be carried forward. In Paula's case she will be able to carry forward £10,000 of unused allowance from 2013/14 and use it in a future tax year.

Earnings Can't Be Carried Forward

Although you can make a pension contribution of up to £190,000 in 2014/15, the contribution you make personally cannot exceed your earnings for the current tax year.

Although you can carry forward unused annual allowance, you cannot carry forward earnings from previous years or make backdated pension contributions.

Membership of a Pension Scheme Required

Unused annual allowance can only be carried forward if you were a member of a registered pension scheme for the year in question.

For example, if you start contributing to a pension in 2014/15 but did not belong to any pension scheme in the three previous tax years, you cannot carry forward any unused annual allowance from those years.

On a practical level, this means that someone who does not currently have a pension plan in place, but may wish to make big contributions in a few years' time, should consider setting one up as soon as possible.

Pension Input Periods

When calculating whether the annual allowance has been exceeded, you do not actually count the pension contributions made during the *tax year* (5 April to 6 April) but rather the pension scheme's annual *pension input period*.

You count a pension input period if it ends during the current tax year. For example, pension contributions during a pension input period that ends on 30 June 2014 count towards the 2014/15 tax year.

It is possible that pension contributions made during two different tax years may fall into just one pension input period. If you're making quite big pension contributions this means you could end up exceeding the annual allowance and face a tax charge.

Example

Joan opened a pension plan with an insurance company on 1 November a few years ago and her annual pension input period runs from 1 November to 31 October each year.

She made a pension contribution of £30,000 on 1 November 2013. This pension input period ends on 31 October 2014.

31 October 2014 falls into the 2014/15 tax year, so Joan's £30,000 contribution is treated as having been made in the 2014/15 tax year when it comes to deciding whether the annual allowance has been exceeded – even though the contribution was actually made during the 2013/14 tax year.

If Joan also contributes £30,000 on 1 June 2014 (i.e., during the same pension input period), this contribution will also fall into the 2014/15 tax year when it comes to deciding if the annual allowance has been exceeded.

In summary, Joan has made pension contributions totalling £60,000 in the pension input period that ends inside the 2014/15 tax year.

This means she has exceeded the annual allowance by £20,000 even though she made the pension contributions in two separate tax years.

In practice, pension input periods are an issue for some but not many pension savers:

- Many pension providers (including many SIPP providers) align the pension input period with the tax year. This means contributions made in two separate tax years will always be treated as having been made in two separate pension input periods.

- For pension schemes set up after 6 April 2011 the default pension input period is the same as the tax year.

- Even if you do exceed the annual allowance the excess may be covered by the carry forward rules.

Getting your Contribution Right

The pension contribution rules are quite complex... but only if you have big contributions and are in danger of exceeding the annual allowance.

Most people will not have anything close to £40,000 added to their pension pots during the current tax year and are completely unaffected by the annual allowance rules (individuals who want to make big catch-up contributions are an important exception – see Chapter 15).

The earnings limit is also irrelevant for the vast majority of people who go out to work each day. Most would never contemplate contributing anything close to 100% of their earnings to a pension. (Company directors are one exception because they often pay themselves a small tax-free salary and therefore have very low 'relevant UK earnings'.)

I don't want to sound flippant but it's important not to become bogged down by rules that may never affect you. Calculating the maximum pension contribution you *can* make is not the important issue for most people. What is far more important is calculating the maximum pension contribution you *should* make.

A far more important calculation for many individuals is the maximum contribution that will obtain full higher-rate tax relief. This is the subject of the next chapter.

Lifetime Allowance

The lifetime allowance is the maximum amount of money you are allowed to save up in pensions. If you exceed the lifetime cap you may have to pay the lifetime allowance charge, which is essentially a tax on people who save hard or make successful investments.

Since 6 April 2014 the lifetime allowance has been set at £1.25 million (previously £1.5 million).

Typically, your pension pot will be tested against the lifetime allowance when you start taking benefits. If you've accumulated, say, £1.5 million of pension savings you may have to pay the lifetime allowance charge on the extra £250,000.

The lifetime allowance charge is 55% if the excess funds are taken as a lump sum, 25% if the excess funds are taken out as taxable income.

The critical question is: "Am I in danger of exceeding the lifetime allowance?"

Although £1.25 million may seem like a lot of money to the average reader, it is possible that the lifetime allowance will be reduced again or simply remain at its current level permanently or for many years, which means its real value will be eroded steadily by inflation.

For example, if you're 35 and currently have more than £70,000 of pension savings, growing at 10% per year, you will exceed the lifetime allowance by the time you are 65, *even if you don't make any more pension contributions.*

Similarly, if you're 45 you will exceed the lifetime allowance by the time you are 65 if you currently have around £190,000 of pension savings.

The problem with doing calculations like these, however, is that the outcome can be altered easily by tweaking the numbers.

For example, if we assume that the two individuals' investments grow by 7% per year, instead of 10%, the 35 year old will only exceed the lifetime allowance at age 65 if he has a pension pot of around £165,000 at present. The 45 year old will only exceed the lifetime allowance at age 65 if he has a pension pot of around £325,000 at present. Again this assumes they make no more pension contributions.

If the two individuals continue making pension contributions there is a more significant danger that the lifetime allowance will be breached.

For example, if we assume that the two individuals' investments grow by 7% per year and they personally contribute £6,000 per year to their pensions, the 35 year old will exceed the lifetime allowance at age 65 if he has a pension pot of around £65,000 at present. The 45 year old will exceed the lifetime allowance at age 65 if he has a pension pot of around £240,000 at present.

In summary, if the lifetime allowance is not increased from its current level of £1.25 million, an increasing number of pension savers will face the danger of exceeding the lifetime allowance.

Those individuals most at risk are the ones who have already accumulated significant pension savings but are still many years away from retirement.

If you think you may be affected by the lifetime allowance, it is essential to speak to a financial advisor about your options.

Chapter 3

How to Maximise Your Higher-Rate Tax Relief

Everyone who makes pension contributions gets basic-rate tax relief (the taxman's 20% top up). If you are a higher-rate taxpayer you can also claim an additional 20% tax relief.

However, many higher-rate taxpayers don't enjoy full tax relief on their pension contributions because they don't understand how higher-rate relief is calculated.

It's a bit like paying for a business class ticket and accidentally sitting in economy.

What is a Higher-Rate Taxpayer?

A higher-rate taxpayer is currently someone who has taxable income of more than £41,865.

How is this number calculated? For most individuals the first £10,000 of income is tax free (this is your income tax personal allowance). The next £31,865 is taxed at 20% (your basic-rate band). Anything over £41,865 is taxed at 40%.

These thresholds are usually changed each year. These are the figures for the 2014/15 tax year.

How Is Higher-Rate Relief Calculated?

When you make pension contributions the taxman gives you a bigger basic-rate band, which means more of your income is taxed at 20% instead of 40%.

Your basic-rate band is increased by the same amount as your *gross* pension contributions.

Example

Sandy is a sole trader with pre-tax profits of £50,000. He has £8,135 of income taxed at 40% (£50,000 - £41,865).

He puts £5,000 into a pension. The taxman adds £1,250 of basic-rate relief for a gross contribution of £6,250 (£5,000/0.8).

To calculate his higher-rate relief his basic-rate band is increased by £6,250, allowing £6,250 of income to be taxed at 20% instead of 40%. This saves Sandy £1,250 in tax (£6,250 x 20%).

This is the best possible outcome. Sandy has received basic-rate and higher-rate tax relief on his entire pension contribution. In total he enjoys 40% tax relief:

$$(£1,250 + £1,250) / £6,250 = 40\%$$

The Maximum Higher Rate Relief

The maximum higher-rate tax relief you can claim is:

Your Gross Pension Contribution x 20%

However, you will only enjoy the maximum higher-rate tax relief if you have at least this much income taxed at 40%.

If your income is £41,865 plus one pound, you can only get higher-rate tax relief on one pound of pension contributions.

Sandy, whose income is £50,000, can get higher-rate tax relief on a gross pension contribution of up to £8,135 (£50,000 – £41,865). His actual gross pension contribution is £6,250 so he has stayed within the limits. If he contributes more than £8,135, the additional contribution will only get basic-rate relief.

Tax Planning

Big pension contributions can be a bad idea if you don't have enough income taxed at 40%.

To enjoy the maximum tax relief you may want to consider spreading your pension contributions over a number of tax years.

26

If maximising tax relief is your priority, you should make sure your gross pension contributions do not exceed the amount of income you have taxed at 40%.

Example revisited

Sandy is a sole trader with pre-tax profits of £50,000. He has £8,135 of income taxed at 40% (£50,000 - £41,865).

This time Sandy puts £15,000 into a pension. The taxman adds £3,750 of basic-rate relief. His gross contribution is £18,750 (£15,000/0.8).

His basic-rate band is increased by £18,750 which means his maximum higher-rate tax relief is:

$$£18,750 \times 20\% = £3,750$$

However, Sandy doesn't have £18,750 of income taxed at 40%, he only has £8,135. So the actual higher-rate relief he will receive is:

$$£8,135 \times 20\% = £1,627$$

Although his basic-rate band has been increased significantly, he doesn't have enough income to use it! Sandy is only obtaining higher-rate tax relief on £8,135 worth of pension contributions. In total he enjoys just 29% tax relief:

$$(£3,750 + £1,627) / £18,750 = 29\%$$

What can Sandy do if he wants to enjoy the maximum higher-rate relief? He could spread his pension contributions over several tax years.

If he wants to invest £15,000 (£18,750 gross) and if we assume he has £8,135 of income per year taxed at 40%, this means he could consider spreading his gross contributions over three tax years:

Year 1	£8,135
Year 2	£8,135
Year 3	£2,480

(The higher-rate threshold changes from year to year, so this is just a rough estimate.)

Table 1
Maximising Higher-Rate Tax Relief:
Maximum Pension Contributions 2014/15

Taxable Income £	Maximum Gross Contribution £	Maximum Net Contribution £
45,000	3,135	2,508
50,000	8,135	6,508
55,000	13,135	10,508
60,000	18,135	14,508
65,000	23,135	18,508
70,000	28,135	22,508
75,000	33,135	26,508
80,000	38,135	30,508
85,000	43,135	34,508
90,000	48,135	38,508
95,000	53,135	42,508
100,000	58,135	46,508

Rule of Thumb

If maximising tax relief is your priority, the maximum amount you should contribute to a pension in the 2014/15 tax year is:

Your taxable income <u>minus</u> *£41,865*

This is your maximum gross pension contribution. Multiply this number by 0.8 to obtain the maximum amount you can actually invest (your net cash contribution).

Table 1 contains some sample maximum pension contributions for different levels of income.

Although you can contribute up to £40,000 per year to a pension (ignoring any employer contributions), only someone with income of at least £81,865 would enjoy full higher-rate tax relief on such a large gross contribution:

£81,865 - £41,865 = £40,000

Someone with income over £81,865 could contribute more than the £40,000 annual allowance and enjoy higher-rate tax relief on the entire contribution. However, to do this they would have to carry forward unused annual allowance from previous tax years.

Big Contributions Close to Retirement

When you are very close to retirement it may be worth making pension contributions that are much larger than you can normally afford, even if you only enjoy basic-rate tax relief on some of your investment.

From April 2015, it will be possible to withdraw all the extra money you contribute immediately after you retire and 25% will be tax free.

We'll take a look at the potential tax savings in Chapter 9.

Pension Input Periods

In the previous chapter I pointed out that, when calculating if the annual allowance has been exceeded, you use pension input periods, not tax years.

Do pension input periods also affect higher-rate relief? For example, let's say you make pension contributions in two separate tax years but they take place in the same pension input period.

Will the contributions be treated for tax relief purposes as having been made in a single tax year? If so, this could result in your higher-rate relief being restricted if you don't have enough income taxed at 40% in that single tax year.

Pension input periods are used to calculate whether the annual allowance has been exceeded but do not have an impact upon higher-rate tax relief.

Tax relief is always granted in the tax year when the contribution was actually made.

Chapter 4

How to Claim Higher-Rate Tax Relief

Approximately 400,000 higher-rate taxpayers do not claim their higher-rate tax relief, losing close to one billion pounds in the process.

Many taxpayers believe incorrectly that all of their pension tax relief is automatically credited to their pension pots.

Those who usually do NOT have to claim higher-rate tax relief are members of occupational money purchase pension schemes. Their pension contributions are paid out of their salaries before tax is deducted, so full 40% tax relief is effectively granted immediately.

Those who are affected include members of group personal pensions, group stakeholder pensions and group SIPPs. With these arrangements the contributions are made out of after-tax pay, so tax relief has to be actively claimed.

Individuals with their own private pension plans also have to actively claim their higher-rate tax relief.

Gross vs Net Contributions

Another mistake made by higher-rate taxpayers when completing tax returns is entering net cash pension contributions (the amount they actually pay in), instead of their gross contributions (which include the taxman's basic-rate tax relief top up).

Page 4 of your tax return is for 'Tax reliefs'. Box 1 asks for:

Payments to registered pension schemes where basic rate tax relief will be claimed by your pension provider (called 'relief at source'). Enter the payments and basic rate tax.

If you personally pay £3,000 into your pension and insert this number on your tax return, the taxman will give you £600 of higher-rate tax relief:

$$£3,000 \times 20\% = £600$$

But if you enter the correct amount, which is £3,750 (£3,000/0.8), the taxman will give you £750 of higher-rate tax relief:

$$£3,750 \times 20\% = £750$$

Do not include employer pension contributions.

Backdated Claims

If you have not claimed your higher-rate tax relief, the good news is you can make a backdated claim going back four years. Rebates can run to thousands of pounds.

Write to your local tax office, outlining the gross contributions you have made and the tax years they relate to, or speak to an accountant.

How to Claim Higher-Rate Tax Relief

The standard way to claim higher-rate tax relief is when you submit your tax return. You can also claim it through an adjustment to your tax code. This allows tax relief to be provided immediately because less tax will be deducted from your salary each month.

(A tax code is used by your employer to calculate the amount of tax to deduct from your pay. If you have the wrong tax code you could end up paying too much tax.)

You can have your tax code adjusted by writing to your tax office and some pension companies provide template letters for this purpose.

You may need to contact HMRC again if your pension contributions increase, for example if you get a pay increase or if you make one-off contributions during the year.

Chapter 5

Higher-Rate Relief: Here to Stay?

The previous Labour Government decided to withdraw higher-rate tax relief from those with income over £150,000. After the last general election there were fresh fears that the new coalition Government would go one step further and scrap higher-rate tax relief for everyone. Some senior members of the Government wanted to do this in the interests of 'fairness'... that word politicians love to bandy around these days.

Fortunately, it was decided that higher-rate tax relief would not be taken away from anyone, even those earning over £150,000. The Government stated that: "Tax relief will be available at an individual's marginal rate." This means that even those who earn over £150,000 and pay 45% tax can enjoy 45% tax relief on their pension contributions.

What the Government has done is restrict the amount that can be paid into a pension. It has done this by reducing the annual allowance, first to £50,000 and now to £40,000.

Could the Government Clamp Down Further?

Yes. In the run up to almost every Budget or Autumn Statement since the coalition government came to power, the Liberal Democrats have called for further cuts to pension tax reliefs.

Fortunately, their most extreme proposals, including the complete abolition of higher-rate tax relief, have been kicked into Room 101 for now. For the current 2014/15 tax year all taxpayers can continue enjoying tax relief at their marginal income tax rate.

However, a restriction to pension tax relief at some point in the years ahead cannot be ruled out.

Personally, I don't think higher-rate tax relief will be taken away completely. Doing so would probably discourage many (if not most) higher-rate taxpayers from using pensions to save for retirement.

However, further attacks on high-income earners (an easy political target) are a distinct possibility. As part of its next election manifesto, the Labour Party has pledged to restrict pension tax relief for people earning over £150,000 to the same rate as basic-rate taxpayers.

A further reduction in the lifetime allowance also cannot be ruled out. The Liberal Democrats favour cutting it from £1.25 million to £1 million.

The bottom line: the tax reliefs enjoyed by pension savers are at the mercy of the Government of the day. A change in policy could result in some of these reliefs being reduced or taken away.

Part 2

The New Pension Rules: Taking Money Out

Chapter 6

Introduction

Before Age 55

At present you cannot withdraw any money from your pension plans until you reach age 55.

In 2028 the minimum age is expected to increase to 57, when the state pension age increases to 67. So if you were born after April 1973, you will have to wait at least another two years before you can tap your savings.

Thereafter the minimum age is expected to increase in line with increases in the state pension age, so that it is always 10 years below state pension age. As a result, the minimum age you can withdraw money from your pension may increase to 58 by the mid 2030s and 59 by the late 2040s.

Furthermore, the Government is also consulting on whether to raise the minimum pension age so that it is always *five years* below state pension age, to force people to save more before retiring.

This is the most significant drawback when it comes to tucking money away inside a pension. There are times when even financially conservative individuals may need to tap their savings before they are 55 or 57 or older. Obvious examples would be to pay unforeseen family medical expenses or a child's education costs. In the worst case scenario you may even need to access your pension savings early to avoid bankruptcy or home repossession.

Before making significant pension contributions you should always make sure you have other resources to protect against:

- Unforeseen expenses, and an
- Unforeseen drop in income.

Although the money sitting in your pension is out of reach until you're at least 55, it's important to stress that the money is often yours to invest as you please. These days many personal pension plans, especially SIPPs, provide enormous investment flexibility.

The Ill Health Exceptions

As it happens, there are two exceptions to the no withdrawals before age 55 rule... but if you are squeamish you should look away now.

Firstly, all pension savings can be withdrawn as a tax-free lump sum if you suffer from "serious ill health" (the polite way of saying you have less than a year to live).

You can also withdraw money from pension plans if you suffer from "ill health" (i.e. you are not about to die but are too sick to work again).

After Age 55

When you reach age 55 (or older in future) you can keep your money growing tax free in your pension for as long as you like or you can start withdrawing it.

Note, however, that this is the minimum age set out in the tax rules. Some company pension schemes stipulate an older retirement age, for example 60, and you may need permission to start withdrawing money earlier.

At present, even when you reach age 55, the amount of money you can withdraw from your pension is tightly controlled. Most individuals' savings can only come out at a trickle, either through an annuity or something called "capped drawdown".

However, this restriction will be lifted shortly following George Osborne's announcement in the March 2014 Budget that:

"We will legislate to remove all remaining tax restrictions on how pensioners have access to their pension pots. Pensioners will have complete freedom to draw down as much or as little of their pension pot as they want, anytime they want. No caps. No drawdown limits. Let me be clear. No one will have to buy an annuity."

This change will give retirees more control over their pension savings than they have ever had and remove one of the biggest obstacles that deters people from using pensions to save for retirement.

You will still have to be 55 or 57 (or perhaps even older) before you can dip into your pension pot. However, you will then be able to withdraw as much money as you like, whenever you like.

Note, the new withdrawal rules will only apply from April 2015 and the Government is currently consulting on the changes.

Although the existing restrictions are still in place, they are largely academic if you haven't reached pension age yet... unless, that is, the Government announces a dramatic volte-face at some point in the coming months (it wouldn't be unheard of).

The proposed reforms will apply to all those with "defined contribution" pension savings, for example those with personal pensions and SIPPs. They are not aimed at members of defined benefit pension schemes, such as final salary schemes.

Although final salary schemes offer attractive benefits, the Government believes that some individuals may still wish to transfer from defined benefit schemes to defined contribution schemes so that they can have greater access to their pension savings.

The Government therefore intends to introduce legislation to prevent public sector employees transferring from final salary pension schemes to defined contribution schemes, except in very limited circumstances.

The Government is also concerned that if large numbers of private sector employees transfer from defined benefit schemes to defined contribution schemes this will have harmful effects on the economy. It is therefore consulting on whether to prevent such transfers or restrict them in some way.

In Chapter 7 we take a very brief look at the existing drawdown rules because they still apply for the current 2014/15 tax year. In Chapter 9 we take a closer look at some of the strategies you may be able to follow in future in order to minimize the tax payable when you withdraw money from your pension.

Tax on Withdrawals

Although you can take one quarter of your pension savings as a tax-free lump sum, you have to pay income tax on everything else you withdraw, *including your original contributions*.

That's like putting £100 in a bank account and paying £20 or maybe £40 tax when you withdraw the money a year later. Of course, this doesn't happen when you withdraw money from your bank account – you only pay tax on your interest income.

So while pensions offer several tax concessions, there is a tax sting at the end.

Thus, the sixty-four-thousand dollar question is this:

Do the tax benefits – tax relief on contributions and tax-free investment growth – outweigh the penalty of heavily taxed withdrawals?

In most cases the answer is "Yes". This is because most people will probably pay no more than 20% tax on the money they take out but will have enjoyed 40% tax relief when they put their money in, if they were higher-rate taxpayers.

Furthermore, some of the money you take out will be tax free, including your tax-free lump sum and any withdrawals that are covered by your income tax personal allowance.

This is why even basic-rate taxpayers will usually also end up better off with a pension. Although they only enjoy 20% tax relief when they put their money in, a significant chunk of the money they take out will be tax free.

But *exactly* how much better off are you likely to be with a pension? The benefits surely have to be significant to justify tying up your money until age 55 or later.

One way to answer this question is to compare two investors: one putting money into a pension and the other putting money into a different tax shelter, an ISA, and see who ends up better off at the end of the day.

We do this in Chapter 12.

Like pensions, money in ISAs grows tax free. However, unlike pensions, ISAs do not offer any upfront tax relief but all your withdrawals are tax free and your money is not tied up until age 55 or later – you can withdraw it whenever you like.

However, the problem with using ISAs as retirement saving vehicles is they give you tax relief when you may need it least.

It's better to have 40% tax relief when you put your money in, as you do with pensions, rather than 20% tax relief when you take it out, as you do with ISAs (most individuals would only pay 20% tax when they retire).

Chapter 7

Flexible Drawdown and Capped Drawdown

For the current 2014/15 tax year if you want to withdraw money from your pension and do not want to buy an annuity you have to use either flexible drawdown or capped drawdown.

Flexible Drawdown

Flexible drawdown places no limits on the amount of money you can withdraw from your pension savings. As long as you are 55 you can extract all your pension savings in one go as a lump sum.

Flexible drawdown is the Rolls Royce of pension drawdown but, like a Rolls Royce, not everyone can currently afford it. To qualify you have to have other income of at least £12,000 (known as the minimum income requirement).

And it's not any old income that qualifies. It has to be pension income from:

- State pensions and other social security pensions
- A pension annuity
- A pension scheme with at least 20 members receiving income
- Certain overseas pensions

Income from other drawdown arrangements does NOT qualify because it is not secure income. Nor does income from rental properties, a share portfolio or other investments.

You could own a £1 million property portfolio which produces £50,000 of income and you will still be barred from flexible drawdown, unless you also have at least £12,000 of secure pension income.

One restriction with flexible drawdown is that you have to stop saving into pensions. All contributions to all your pension arrangements must stop permanently in the tax year in which you start flexible drawdown. Any subsequent contributions will be subject to the annual allowance charge.

Capped Drawdown

Capped drawdown is flexible drawdown's somewhat plainer sister. With capped drawdown the idea is you take 25% of your pension savings as a tax-free lump sum but leave the remaining 75% invested (e.g. in shares, commercial property, bonds and cash).

Regular but restricted withdrawals are made from the remaining 75%. As with flexible drawdown, all withdrawals over and above the 25% lump sum are fully taxed.

If your investments perform well you will be able to increase your retirement income over time. If your investments perform badly, your retirement income will fall and could be depleted.

As with flexible drawdown, there's no minimum withdrawal: You can choose to withdraw nothing in any given tax year. Alternatively, you could withdraw just the income generated by your investments (dividends, interest, rental income etc) or you can dip into your capital if you want to boost your income.

Although there is no minimum income, there is a **maximum** income. This is the key difference between flexible and capped drawdown.

The cap is designed to protect you from depleting your retirement savings if you don't have a £12,000 cushion from other pensions (the minimum income for flexible drawdown).

The maximum income you can take is based on the annuity payable to a person your age. It is calculated using tables from the Government Actuary Department (the so-called GAD tables). You can download the spreadsheet containing the drawdown pension tables from a link on this web page:

www.hmrc.gov.uk/pensionschemes/gad-tables.htm

There is one table for men and one table for women. However, since December 2012 pension companies and others have been prevented from discriminating according to gender, so the table for women is now irrelevant and everyone should use the higher male rates. The third table for "pensioners aged under 23" is for dependants' pensions and can also be ignored in most cases.

Using the GAD Table

If you examine the table you will notice it contains a bunch of numbers like £55, £66 etc. The number that applies to you depends on two things:

- Your age
- The interest rate on 15 year Government bonds

The older you are, the more income you can withdraw from your pension because your life expectancy falls as you get older.

The correct Government bond interest rate to use is published on many insurance company websites. Just type "GAD interest rates" into a search engine like Google. It usually changes from month to month.

Let's assume you are 65 years old and the current GAD interest rate is 3%. According to the spreadsheet, the number to use is £59.

Up until fairly recently £59 would have been the maximum amount of income you could withdraw per £1,000 of your pension savings.

However, in the last couple of Budgets the Government has increased the maximum withdrawal to help income-starved retirees. In the most recent March 2014 Budget, the Government decided to let capped drawdown users withdraw an extra 50% over and above the maximum set out in the tables.

So if the relevant number in the table is £59, multiply this by 1.5 to get £88.50 which is the maximum you can currently withdraw per £1,000 of your pension savings.

So someone with a £100,000 pension pot, after taking their tax-free lump sum, could take a maximum income of £8,850 during the current tax year.

This is the so-called "150% of GAD" you sometimes read about in the financial press.

Small Pension Pots

If you are 60 or over and have total pension savings of £30,000 or less you can currently take this as a lump sum (the limit was £18,000 before 27 March 2014). 25% is tax free and the rest is taxed at your marginal rate of income tax.

The maximum size of a small pension pot which can be taken as a lump sum, regardless of total pension savings, has also been increased from £2,000 to £10,000, and the number of personal pots that can be taken under these rules has been increased from two to three.

Old Drawdown & vs Pension Freedom

The existing system of flexible and capped drawdown will operate until 6 April 2015. From that date the new pension withdrawal rules will hopefully come into operation.

Essentially the Government is proposing that everyone will be able to use flexible drawdown, without requiring £12,000 of secure pension income.

Most retirees will, however, probably be advised (but not compelled) to base their pension withdrawals on the capped drawdown system, which limits the amount you take out according to your age and life expectancy.

No doubt many pension companies will develop new products based on this system to help retirees withdraw money responsibly.

Chapter 8

What Happens When You Die?

If you are going to be saving lots of money in pensions, you need to know what will happen to your money when you die. Will it go to the people that matter (your family) or will it be gobbled up by the Government or an insurance company or pension firm?

The answer depends on a number of factors including your age when you die, whether you've started withdrawing money already and whether you have 'dependants'.

After you die, your remaining pension savings will normally be used to continue paying a pension to your spouse or another financial dependant (e.g. a common-law spouse). When they die any remaining pension drawdown money will probably be paid out as lump sum to your children, after deducting a 'recovery tax', currently 55%.

The Government believes that a flat 55% tax rate will be too high in future given that everyone with defined contribution pension savings (including basic-rate taxpayers) will be able to use drawdown rather than buy an annuity. However, we don't know by how much it will be reduced at this stage.

There will normally be nothing left for your children if an annuity has been purchased in place of income drawdown. Does this mean drawdown arrangements are better than annuities? No. If you live longer than average you could receive a lot more money from an annuity because the income is guaranteed for life and is never reduced.

Death **before** Taking Benefits

There are two rules, depending on whether you are:

- Under 75 years of age
- 75 or older

If you are under 75 and die *before* taking benefits from your pension, all of your pension savings can be paid out tax free to family members or other beneficiaries.

This is why some financial advisors recommend something called 'phased drawdown' before age 75 – a gradual rather than total transfer of pension savings into drawdown. If you die before age 75, the part of your pension pot you have not started drawing money out of (the 'uncrystallised' portion) can be bequeathed as a totally tax-free lump sum.

If you are 75 or over, the 55% tax is currently payable on lump sums paid to family members. However, this can be avoided if your pension savings are used instead to provide a 'dependant's pension'. This pension will be subject to income tax. The dependant's pension can take the form of an annuity or the money can be kept in a drawdown arrangement where it can continue to grow tax free.

Note, not all family members are dependants. Dependants would normally include:

- Your spouse or unmarried partner (common-law spouse)
- Children under the age of 23
- Any other person considered your financial dependant

Death after Taking Benefits

Annuities
If you have used your pension savings to purchase a joint-life annuity, income will continue to be paid to the second person after you die (normally your spouse or partner).

You can also buy an annuity that pays income for a guaranteed period, e.g. 10 years, so if you die after two years income will continue to be paid out for another 8 years.

Without these or other special features (which cost money) your family members will receive nothing after you die.

Drawdown

If your pension savings are in a drawdown arrangement when you die, all of the remaining money can be paid out as a cash lump sum to your nominated beneficiaries. There will, however, be a recovery tax charge (currently 55%).

This tax can be avoided if the money is used to provide a dependant's pension, if you have a spouse, partner of children under 23 years of age. The dependant's pension can take the form of an annuity or can be kept in a drawdown arrangement.

When the dependant dies the leftover funds can be paid out as a lump sum to other family members, eg adult children, after deducting the recovery tax charge (currently 55%).

Pensions and Inheritance Tax

When you die it is possible to pass your pension savings to your family or other beneficiaries free from inheritance tax. This means pensions are *potentially* useful inheritance tax shelters in some circumstances.

Lump sum death benefits can be passed on free from inheritance tax if the pension scheme trustees have discretion as to who will receive the death benefits. You can nominate a beneficiary and the trustees of the pension scheme will probably act in accordance with your wishes ... but they are not legally bound by them. This means your pension savings are not actually your property when your estate is valued.

Although the recovery tax may be deducted from lump sum payments on your death (where no dependant's pension is paid), this tax is supposed to recover the tax relief added to your pension pot over the years and is not an inheritance tax charge.

There are some inheritance tax charges that apply to pensions, eg where certain contributions are made within two years of death whilst the member was in ill health.

In Chapter 13 we will take a closer look at how ISAs and pensions compare when it comes to saving inheritance tax.

Chapter 9

Pension Freedom: How Retirees May Be Able to Save Tax

When the pension rules are relaxed in April 2015 a few reckless individuals will probably squander their pension savings on Lamborghinis. The vast majority will withdraw their money gradually and spend it wisely.

Nevertheless, there is still a danger that even careful retirees will spend their savings a bit too quickly and end up depleting their pension pots.

Those who want a guaranteed income for life, with no danger of running out of money, can always hand over their retirement savings to an annuity provider. For example, a 65 year old with a £200,000 pension pot can currently buy a guaranteed income for life of £6,000 per year. This income will increase in line with inflation and continue providing a pension for their widow.

It's not a lot but then again annuity rates are abnormally low at present because interest rates are so low. It may be possible to achieve a higher income by using a drawdown arrangement and investing in, for example, companies with a long track record of paying growing dividends, or other investments.

With drawdown you don't have to hand over your retirement savings to an annuity provider but then again your income is not guaranteed and could fall, as could the value of your investments.

This is the dilemma retirees will face in the wake of George Osborne's pensions revolution. Freedom to hold onto your pension pot will not necessarily buy you peace of mind when you're spending it.

There's no doubt that insurance companies and other pension companies will dream up all sorts of clever products to help retirees invest and spend their pension savings prudently, perhaps along the lines of the existing capped drawdown arrangements we discussed in Chapter 7, but with fewer restrictions.

Either way, you should only spend a fraction of your pension pot each year if your savings are to last through your retirement.

Some retirees may, however, wish to make bigger than normal withdrawals and that doesn't necessarily mean they're going to fritter the money away. For example, you could use it to:

- Invest tax free in ISAs
- Buy rental property
- Reduce your mortgage or other debts
- Start a business

Another reason retirees may wish to withdraw their money as quickly as possible is to avoid the 55% recovery tax that is payable on your remaining pension savings when you die (see Chapter 8). However, the Government believes this tax is too high and is currently consulting on reducing it.

Tax will be an extremely important factor when it comes to deciding how much you withdraw from your pension and when. In this chapter we're going to take a closer look at some of the strategies pension savers may be able to follow to pay less income tax and capital gains tax.

For the first time, pension savers will have the freedom to control their tax bills to some extent, by making big pension withdrawals in some tax years and smaller withdrawals in others.

Saving Income Tax

Any money you withdraw from your pension, over and above your 25% tax-free lump sum, is subject to income tax. If you withdraw a lot in one go, you could end up paying tax at 40% or even 45%.

Most retirees should endeavour to pay no more than 20% tax on any money they withdraw from their pension pots and one way to achieve this is by spreading withdrawals over many tax years.

In 2015/16, when the new pension withdrawal rules come into operation, you will pay no more than 20% tax as long as your total taxable income from all sources is less than £42,285.

The first £10,500 will be tax free and the remaining £31,785 will be taxed at 20%. Any additional income will be taxed at 40% and possibly 45%.

Most retirees do not, on average, earn more than £42,285 and should therefore refrain from making big pension withdrawals that push them into the 40% tax bracket.

Example

It's the start of the 2015/16 tax year. Andrew is 60 and earns a salary of £50,000. He has been saving into a personal pension and ISA. His pension pot is worth £200,000 and his ISA savings are worth £100,000. His wife Elizabeth is the same age and has similar income and savings.

If Andrew withdraws all of his pension savings in one go, one quarter (£50,000) would be tax free. The remaining £150,000 would be fully taxed. His total taxable income would be £200,000 (£50,000 salary plus £150,000 pension).

With this much income, Andrew would not be entitled to any personal allowance which means an additional £10,500 of his salary would be taxed at 40%. Turning to his pension, £100,000 would be taxed at 40% and the remaining £50,000 at 45%. His total income tax bill will rise from £9,443 (salary only) to £76,143. Andrew ends up paying tax at an effective rate of 44% on his pension withdrawal.

Furthermore, the money he takes out will no longer grow tax free outside his pension.

Andrew realizes that he is better off leaving his pension savings alone while he is working full time. He doesn't even want to withdraw his tax-free lump sum because he has no use for the money at present and wants it to continue growing tax free.

In fact, instead of taking money out, he intends to keep putting as much money as possible into both his pension and ISA out of his salary.

This is another reason why pension savers may need to be careful about tapping their savings too early. Under the current rules, you are effectively prevented from making any further pension contributions to any pension scheme ever again after going into flexible drawdown. A similar rule may operate from April 2015.

Example continued

Three years later when he's 63 Andrew resigns from his job because he wants to work part time. His pension pot is now worth £270,000 and his ISA savings are worth £175,000. Before getting a part-time job he decides to take a year off to pursue various interests, including buying and renovating a rental property. Andrew and Elizabeth withdraw 25% of their pension lump sums tax free to fund the purchase of the property (£135,000 in total).

Although the property will produce <u>taxable</u> income and capital gains (whereas the money was growing tax free before they took out of their pensions), Andrew and Elizabeth believe they have found a genuine bargain which makes up for the loss of tax relief.

Because he has no other taxable income, Andrew also decides to withdraw an additional £10,500 tax free so as not to waste his income tax personal allowance for the year. He could also withdraw an additional amount of up to £31,785 which would be taxed at just 20% (using 2015/16 tax rates for simplicity).

Example continued

A year later Andrew is now 64 and gets a part-time job, earning £15,000 per year. He's also earning £5,000 of rental income from his share of the property. If he doesn't need any more income he can leave his pension pot alone and let it grow tax free.

If he does want to withdraw some money he can take up to £22,285 taxed at just 20% (again using 2015/16 tax rates for simplicity).

Two years later Andrew is 66 and has reached state pension age and decides to stop working. His pension pot is now worth around £240,000 and his ISA savings have grown to around £210,000. Coupled with Elizabeth's savings and the income from the rental property, he feels financially secure enough to retire.

His state pension and rental income use up his income tax personal allowance so he will pay at least 20% tax on any amounts he withdraws from his pension in the future He therefore decides to withdraw an additional £20,000 per year but doesn't necessarily spend all of that money.

Reducing Capital Gains Tax

Because retirees will be free from April 2015 to choose how much money they withdraw from their pension pots each year, they will be able to halt or reduce withdrawals in years they sell assets like rental property and reduce their capital gains tax bills.

This is because you only pay 18% capital gains tax (as opposed to 28%) to the extent that your basic-rate band is not used up by your income. For example, in 2015/16 if you don't have any taxable income you can have £31,785 of capital gains taxed at 18%.

The potential tax saving is £6,357 per couple:

$$£31,785 \text{ x } 2 \text{ x } 10\% = £6,357$$

Example continued

Several years later Andrew and Elizabeth decide to sell their rental property because it has increased in value significantly and they don't want the hassle of managing tenants etc. They intend to use the proceeds to buy a holiday cottage.

After deducting various buying and selling costs and their annual CGT exemptions they expect to be left with taxable capital gains of £30,000 each. These amounts will be taxed at just 18%, providing they haven't withdrawn too much income from their pension pots.

In the tax year before the sale takes place they therefore decide to make larger than normal withdrawals from their pension pots, making sure they stay below the higher-rate threshold to avoid paying 40% tax.

In the tax year in which the property is sold they reduce their pension withdrawals so that all of their capital gains will be taxed at 18%. They live off the extra income they withdrew during the previous tax year.

Once the sale has taken place, and they know how much of their basic-rate bands are left, they can withdraw some additional money from their pension pots taxed at just 20%.

Leaving Pension Wealth to Your Family

When you die your remaining pension savings can be left to your family after deducting a recovery tax (currently 55% but expected to be significantly reduced from April 2015).

However, if your remaining savings are used to provide a dependant's pension (typically for your spouse or partner) there is no tax charge. The pension pot can continue growing tax free while money is extracted.

Example continued

When Andrew dies at age 85 his remaining pension savings are left to Elizabeth. She also receives his remaining ISA savings but these cannot be kept in an ISA wrapper after Andrew's death so any income they generate will be taxable.

Elizabeth doesn't need a huge amount of income but withdraws as much money as possible taxed at 20% from Andrews's pension pot and gives it to her children.

Withdrawing Lump Sums Gradually

Under the new pension rules, retirees who wish to make occasional large lump sum withdrawals should try to spread them over more than one tax year wherever possible.

Example

Barbara normally has taxable income of £30,000 made up of her state pension and withdrawals from her personal pension. In 2015/16 she wants to withdraw an additional £25,000 to pay for a new conservatory.

If she withdraws all the money in 2015/16, £12,715 of the additional withdrawal will be taxed at 40%. If she spreads her withdrawals over two tax years just £430 will be taxed at 40%. Her total tax saving is £2,457.

Big Contributions Close to Retirement

Because retirees will shortly be able to make unlimited pension withdrawals, it may be worth making big pension contributions when you are very close to retirement, even if you only enjoy basic-rate tax relief.

Although the money will be taxed when you withdraw it again, 25% of the amount you withdraw will be tax free.

Example
Emily intends to retire during the 2016/17 tax year. She earns a salary of £50,000 and in recent years has been investing just enough into her pension to maximise her higher-rate tax relief (see Chapter 3).

A few years ago she inherited some money from her mother and currently has around £35,000 sitting in the bank earning very little interest. She decides to invest most of it in her pension during 2015/16, the tax year before she retires. She does this in the knowledge that, under the new pension withdrawal rules, she can withdraw all the money immediately after she retires.

During the 2015/16 tax year her normal gross pension contribution is £7,715 (£50,000 salary - £42,285 higher-rate threshold) and this attracts full higher-rate tax relief.

Just before the end of the tax year she invests an additional £33,828. The taxman adds £8,457 of basic-rate tax relief to her pension pot, resulting in an additional gross pension contribution of £42,285. There is no higher-rate tax relief on this additional contribution.

Her total gross pension contributions for 2015/16 come to £50,000 and therefore do not exceed her earnings. They do, however, exceed the £40,000 annual allowance but this isn't a problem because she can use unused allowance from the three previous tax years.

Soon after retiring in 2016/17 she decides to withdraw all of the additional contribution she made in the previous tax year. With tax relief the total sum is £42,285. One quarter (£10,571) can be taken tax free. Emily pays 20% tax on the remaining £31,714.

After tax Emily is left with £35,942, compared with the £33,828 she invested originally. So Emily enjoys a £2,114 windfall from this simple piece of tax planning.

Retirees with Other Income

If you have significant taxable income from other sources (e.g. rental property) and expect this income and your pension pot to grow faster than inflation, it may be worthwhile withdrawing income from your pension early on to avoid paying tax at 40% in future years.

Example
Michael is 55 and owns a portfolio of rental properties with his wife Lorraine. Michael's share of the rental income is £25,000. He doesn't have any other taxable income (he recently stopped working to focus on managing his investments). He also has a pension pot worth £200,000 and ISAs worth £200,000.

Michael is currently a basic-rate taxpayer which means that, during the 2015/16 tax year, he can withdraw £17,285 from his pension and pay just 20% tax (£42,285 higher-rate threshold less £25,000 rental income).

Michael doesn't need this much income but decides to withdraw as much money as he can taxed at 20% and do the same again during future tax years. He does this for two reasons:

Firstly, he realizes that he will <u>always</u> pay at least 20% income tax on any money he withdraws from his pension (because his rental income will always use up his personal allowance). Furthermore, he can invest all of his after-tax pension withdrawals in an ISA so that it continues to grow tax free. Essentially, he loses nothing by shifting his money from one tax shelter to another.

The second reason he makes big withdrawals is because he expects to become a higher-rate taxpayer in the future. Although the higher-rate threshold increases each year in line with inflation, Michael expects his taxable rental income to grow faster than inflation, as he pays off his remaining buy-to-let mortgages, and he expects his pension pot to grow significantly faster than inflation because he is a skilled investor.

Furthermore, at the start of the 2026/27 tax year, when he's 66, he will start receiving his state pension and this will further eat into his basic-rate band. As a result, some of Michael's future pension withdrawals could be taxed at 40%.

For example, let's say inflation is 3% per year but Michael's taxable rental income increases by 5% per year and his pension pot grows by 10% per year. In 2026/27 he'll have rental income of roughly £43,000 and a state pension of possibly £10,000 per year. His total taxable income will be £53,000. The higher-rate threshold could be roughly £58,000 by then which means Michael will only be able to withdraw £5,000 from his pension taxed at 20%. Anything else he withdraws will be taxed at 40%.

By then Michael's pension pot, after he has withdrawn his 25% tax-free lump sum, will have grown to roughly £428,000. If he withdraws pension income of just 5%, he will have additional taxable income of £21,400. Of this, £16,400 (£21,400 - £5,000) will be taxed at 40%, leaving him with just £13,840.

By contrast, if from the age of 55 Michael withdraws as much income as possible from his pension taxed at 20%, by the time he reaches state pension age he will have roughly £80,000 left in his pension pot. If he then withdraws say 5%, he will have additional taxable income of just £4,000 all taxed at just 20%, leaving him with £3,200.

Although Michael has depleted most of his pension pot, the money he has taken out each year has not been frittered away. It has all been invested in an ISA. By the time he reaches state pension age he will have additional ISA savings of £278,000 from which he can make tax free withdrawals.

If he withdraws say 5% he will have additional tax-free income of £13,900. Coupled with his after-tax pension income of £3,200 he is left with £17,100, compared with the £13,840 he would end up with from his pension if he did not start withdrawing money early on.

In summary, Michael enjoys a £3,200 boost to his retirement income, with similar gains possible in every future year.

Tax Danger

At present the Government is consulting on the changes to the pension withdrawal rules. There is a danger that it will perform a u-turn, as governments often do after making generous changes to tax legislation. It's also possible that anti-avoidance rules of some description will be introduced. For this reason it is probably unwise to take any action yet based on the proposed changes.

Summary

- From 2015/16 it will be possible to make unlimited pension withdrawals when you reach pension age (55 or 57 but possibly older).

- Any money you withdraw, over and above your tax-free lump sum, will be subject to income tax.

- Most retirees pay no more than 20% tax and should avoid making withdrawals taxed at 40% or even 45%.

- This can be achieved by spreading withdrawals over many tax years, while keeping an eye on the higher-rate threshold (£42,285 in 2015/16).

- Lump sum withdrawals should be spread over more than one tax year where practical.

- In most cases it will not be tax efficient to withdraw money if you are still working and a higher-rate taxpayer.

- In some cases it may be worth postponing withdrawals so that capital gains are taxed at 18% instead of 28%.

- Money left inside your pension pot when you die will be subject to a recovery tax charge (currently 55%).

- This tax charge can be avoided if your remaining pension savings are used to provide a pension for your spouse. The pension savings will continue to grow tax free, unlike ISAs which have their tax exempt status taken away on death.

Chapter 10

Drawdown vs Annuities

When you retire you may prefer to use your retirement savings to buy an annuity, rather than use drawdown (the type of pension withdrawal arrangement discussed in the previous chapter).

According to the Government, 75% of pension savers currently purchase an annuity. This number is likely to fall dramatically when drawdown becomes more widely available.

Annuities get a bad rap in the press but offer one important benefit: a guaranteed income for life. This may appeal to older retirees who don't want the hassle of managing investments and desire what is as close as it gets to a risk-free income.

Annuity rates are very low at present but may improve if interest rates increase from their current historic lows. Having said this, they may become even less attractive in future if only a small minority of retirees buy them (those who expect to live a long time).

Annuities are seen by many as a con. The idea is lots of retirees pool their money together and those that live longer than average are subsidized by those who live shorter than average. That's fair enough but what many people suspect is that annuity providers (typically insurance companies) skim off a big chunk of the money for themselves.

There are several other reasons why drawdown may be more attractive than buying an annuity:

Benefit #1 – Take the Tax-free Cash and Keep Working

When you reach age 55 you may want to get your hands on your 25% tax-free lump sum but keep working for another 10 years or even longer.

Any additional income you take from your pension pot while you are still working (e.g. an annuity) could be taxed at 40% or more if you also have income from a job or business.

Because there is no minimum income requirement with pension drawdown arrangements, you can postpone further withdrawals until you actually retire and your income tax rate falls.

While you are working your pension savings will continue to grow tax free, although you may be restricted from making any more pension contributions.

Benefit #2 – Keep Your Favourite Investments

If you opt for an annuity you generally have to sell your pension investments and hand over your savings to an insurance company.

This is not an attractive proposition if you are confident your pension investments will perform well.

With a drawdown pension you can enjoy the best of both worlds: an income and tax-free investment growth on the money left inside your pension.

Benefit #3 – Wait for Better Annuity Rates

Many pension experts argue that you should ultimately use your pension savings to buy an annuity because the income is more secure than drawdown income (the income never falls no matter how long you live and no matter what happens to interest rates and the value of investments).

The problem is that annuity rates may be very low when you retire if interest rates are very low, as they are now. One solution is to start your retirement with a drawdown pension and make a phased exit by using part of your drawdown money to buy an annuity at regular intervals if interest rates rise and annuities become more attractive.

Benefit #4 – Reduce Your Income and Save Tax

If you can vary your income from year to year, as you can with drawdown, you can do a lot of constructive tax planning. This is very useful in years when your tax bill may spike because you receive big one-off receipts such as capital gains.

Let's say you sell a buy-to-let property and the capital gain is £50,000. If you reduce your drawdown income in the same tax year, so that your basic-rate band is not fully utilised, you will pay 18% tax instead of 28% tax on a big chunk of your capital gain. For example, you could withdraw just enough income from your pension so that your income tax personal allowance is fully utilised (£10,500 in 2015/16).

The basic-rate band for 2015/16 is £31,785 so the maximum potential tax saving from paying 18% capital gains tax instead of 28% tax would be:

$$£31,785 \times 10\% = £3,179$$

This tax saving could be enjoyed every time you sell a rental property and allows individuals with many properties to wind down their portfolios slowly when they retire.

Further capital gains tax savings can be achieved by spreading property sales across several tax years because this lets you make use of more than one annual CGT exemption. The potential additional tax saving in 2015/16 is £3,108 (£11,100 x 28%).

Part 3

Pensions vs ISAs

Chapter 11

Introduction

Which is better: an ISA or a pension?

This is an important question. ISAs and pensions are the two most popular savings vehicles for individuals.

When it comes to saving tax there are no ifs, buts or maybes: pensions are a **much** more powerful tax shelter.

With ISAs there is no up-front tax relief on the money you put in but withdrawals are tax free. With pensions there is up-front tax relief but most withdrawals are taxed.

At first glance the two tax reliefs appear quite different but, as it happens, tax-free withdrawals (ISAs) and up-front tax relief (pensions), produce exactly the same result, even though the tax savings are enjoyed at different points in time.

However, there are two reasons why pensions are a much better tax shelter:

- **The tax-free lump sum**. Not all of your pension withdrawals are taxed. You can take one quarter as a tax-free lump sum.

- **Retirees pay less tax**. If your tax rate falls from 40% to 20% when you retire – as with most people – a pension will save you more tax than an ISA. Tax-free ISA withdrawals are only as good as tax-relief on pension contributions IF your income tax rate does not fall when you retire.

Thanks to these two factors, it is quite possible that a pension will generate at least 40% more after-tax income than an ISA, as we shall see in the next chapter.

Other Tax Differences

Apart from these major tax differences, pensions and ISAs are treated differently in other respects which may be important in some circumstances.

Interest on Cash Balances

While it has always been possible to hold cash in a stocks and shares ISA, any interest has in effect been paid net of basic-rate tax. Interest earned in a pension is always tax free.

From July 2014 this will change when the new £15,000 ISA allowance is extended to cash ISAs (up until now the cash ISA limit has been half the full allowance for stocks and shares). Interest on cash held in a stocks and shares ISA will then be completely tax-free.

Tax When You Emigrate

If you become non-UK resident your income and capital gains sheltered inside an ISA will continue to be tax free. Tax free in the UK, that is. The amounts may be taxed in your new country of residence. For example, the Isle of Man Government specifically states in its tax return booklet that an ISA's tax-free status "does not apply in the Isle of Man and you should declare any income from these products".

The tax-exempt status of pensions, on the other hand, is recognized in most countries, although they are arguably less portable assets (you can withdraw all your ISA savings easily if you emigrate).

Withholding Taxes on Dividends

These days it is easy for stock market investors to buy shares in overseas companies, the most popular being US companies. You have to be careful about doing this because the dividends are often subject to a withholding tax.

In the US, the dividend withholding tax rate is 30%. However, in terms of the double tax agreement between the US and UK, the amount of withholding tax can be reduced by completing an IRS form W-8BEN. Most online stockbrokers will handle these forms on your behalf so the process is relatively simple.

However, there is an important difference between US shares held inside a pension and an ISA. The double tax agreement provides a specific exemption for pension schemes, which means US dividends can be received tax free by UK pension savers.

The double tax agreement does not, however, recognize ISAs. ISA investors enjoy the same reduced withholding tax rate as everyone else: 15%.

ISAs – Protection from Greedy Politicians

Although pensions are a better tax shelter, one tax benefit unique to ISAs is protection from future increases in tax rates.

Money withdrawn from ISAs is tax free, whether those withdrawals take place next year or in 30 years' time. In contrast, if a future UK Government decides to increase income tax rates or reduce the threshold where 40% tax kicks in, it is quite possible that you will pay more than 20% tax on the money you withdraw from a pension.

It is impossible to predict what will happen to income tax rates in the years ahead. However, there's no denying that Britain has had its fair share of barmy taxes. In 1974, the top income tax rate on earnings was increased to 83% and the top rate on investment income was 98%.

Do you trust politicians not to increase your income tax at any time between now and the date you die? If not, then it may be a good idea to put some of your retirement savings into ISAs.

ISAs are not, however, completely immune from politicians. There have been rumours in the press in recent times about a lifetime cap being placed on ISA savings to limit the number of 'ISA millionaires.' Nothing has been announced to date.

ISAs – Non-tax Benefits

- **Flexibility.** ISAs are extremely flexible investments that allow you to access your savings *at any time*. Pension savers can only access their money when they reach age 55 or 57 (potentially later in future). It's a fat lot of good having £100,000 sitting in your pension pot if you desperately need emergency cash.

- **No age limit**. You cannot keep contributing to a pension indefinitely. Once you reach age 75 you have to stop (although this restriction may be lifted in the near future). There is no upper age limit for ISA investments and you can withdraw money and make new contributions continually.

- **No earnings required.** If you want to contribute more than £3,600 per year to a pension you need 'earnings'. There is no such restriction on ISA investments, although the maximum investment is capped at £15,000 from July 2014.

Pensions – Non-tax Benefits

- **Investment limits.** The maximum pension investment is currently £40,000 and the carry-forward rules allow a contribution of up to £190,000. However, as we saw in Chapter 3, the maximum contribution that you can make with full higher-rate tax relief is probably a lot lower than these limits.

- **Investment choice**. Pensions offer a wider choice of investments than ISAs. For example, ISAs cannot be used to invest directly in commercial property whereas pensions can.

- **Protection from creditors**. In the event of bankruptcy, your savings in an HMRC approved pension cannot be claimed by your creditors. (Most occupational and personal pensions are HMRC approved.) Pension withdrawals can, however, be grabbed if they take place before you are discharged from bankruptcy.

Chapter 12

Case Study: ISA vs Pension

In this chapter we'll follow two investors building up a retirement nest egg over 10 years and see who ends up better off:

- Peter – Pension investor
- Ian – ISA investor

Both are higher-rate taxpayers and invest £6,000 per year. Peter makes an initial contribution of £8,000 to which the taxman adds a further £2,000 in basic-rate tax relief.

He then claims back £2,000 when completing his tax return. All in all Peter has £10,000 of pension savings that have only cost him £6,000.

Ian also invests £6,000 per year out of his own pocket in an ISA. He doesn't get any tax relief on his contributions so his total investment is just £6,000.

Both Peter and Ian enjoy investment returns of 7% per year. These returns are completely tax free for both the ISA investor and the pension investor.

We track how both investors perform from year to year in Table 2. At the end of year 1 they have £10,700 and £6,420 respectively, which is simply their initial investments of £10,000 and £6,000 plus 7% tax-free investment growth.

After five years, Peter has £24,613 more than Ian and after 10 years he has £59,134 more than Ian. Even though they're both earning an identical tax-free return of 7% and investing the same amount of money out of their own pockets, Peter is much better off because his annual investment is boosted by income tax relief on his contributions.

In fact, Ian always has just 60% as much money as Peter. Peter's extra 40% is thanks to the income tax relief he receives on his pension contributions.

Table 2
Pension Savings vs ISA Savings

End Year	Pension £	ISA £
1	10,700	6,420
2	22,149	13,289
3	34,399	20,640
4	47,507	28,504
5	61,533	36,920
6	76,540	45,924
7	92,598	55,559
8	109,780	65,868
9	128,164	76,899
10	147,836	88,702

Income Comparison

Although Ian's retirement savings are much smaller than Peter's, that's not the whole story. Firstly, Ian enjoyed much more flexibility along the way and would have been able to withdraw money from his ISA at any time. Peter can only withdraw money from his pension when he's 55 or older.

Secondly, Ian can withdraw all his ISA savings *tax-free*. Peter will have to pay income tax on any money he withdraws over and above his 25% tax-free lump sum. If he withdraws all his pension savings in one go (which will be possible from April 2015), he will end up paying tax at 40% on most of the money.

However, because these are *retirement savings*, we will assume that both Peter and Ian withdraw only a little bit of money each year, let's say 7%, to avoid depleting their capital too quickly.

Most financial advisors would probably argue that even 7% is too much if Peter and Ian are young retirees and want to protect their incomes from inflation. However, when trying to decide which tax shelter is better, what generally matters most is that Peter and Ian withdraw money at the same rate, rather than the rate itself.

40% Tax, No Tax-Free Lump Sum

To start with we'll pretend that the pension rules do not let Peter take a tax-free lump sum and that he is a higher-rate taxpayer when he retires. His after-tax pension would be:

£147,836 x 7% less 40% tax = £6,209

Ian's ISA income will be:

£88,702 x 7% less 0% tax = £6,209

As you can see their after-tax incomes are *identical*. As I pointed out in the previous chapter, if you are a higher-rate taxpayer both before and after you retire, and ignoring the tax-free lump sum, ISAs and pensions offer identical tax savings.

Peter may have received 40% income tax relief on the money he put in but he also has to pay 40% tax on the money he takes out. This puts him back in the same position as Ian the ISA investor.

40% Tax, Tax-Free Lump Sum

Of course, in practice Peter can take a 25% tax-free lump sum of £36,959 (£147,836 x 25%). We'll assume that he invests it in an ISA to produce some tax-free retirement income.

(In practice, it may take more than one tax year to get the money into an ISA, although he may be able to use any spouse or partner's ISA allowance to speed the process up. To keep things simple we'll assume the whole £36,959 is invested in one go.)

Peter's after-tax income will be:

Pension: £110,877 x 7% less 40% tax = £4,657
ISA: £36,959 x 7% less   0% tax = £2,587

Peter's total income is now £7,244 compared with Ian's ISA income of £6,209.

This means Peter has approximately 17% more income.

In conclusion, even if you are a higher-rate taxpayer when you retire you will still receive more after-tax income from a pension than an ISA, thanks to the tax-free lump sum.

Although most retirees are basic-rate taxpayers, you could end up paying tax at 40% on some or all of your pension if you have a significant amount of income from other sources, e.g. rental property.

20% Tax, Tax-Free Lump Sum

Finally we'll assume that Peter and Ian, like most other retirees, are basic-rate taxpayers when they retire. Peter's after-tax retirement income will be:

Pension: £110,877 x 7% less 20% tax = £6,209
ISA: £36,959 x 7% less 0% tax = £2,587

Peter's total after-tax income is now £8,796. Ian's ISA income is still £6,209.

This means Peter ends up with 42% more income.

By the way, don't be put off by the paltry amounts of income Peter and Ian earn. Remember, we're looking at retirement savings accumulated over a very short time period here – just 10 years – and Peter and Ian do not increase the amount they save each year to compensate for inflation.

The purpose of this case study is to look at the *percentage difference* between the two individuals' retirement incomes.

If we looked at Peter and Ian over a much longer period, say 20 or 30 years, and increased the amount they saved each year, they would of course end up with a far more respectable level of income.

As long as Peter's income is not high enough to take him into the 40% tax bracket (currently £41,865) the percentage difference between his and Ian's income will remain the same.

Alternative Use of Tax-Free Lump Sum

Let's take a look at an alternative but realistic financial planning scenario. Let's assume that Peter does not invest his £36,959 tax-free lump in an ISA but instead uses it to pay off the outstanding mortgage on his home (perhaps he is worried that interest rates will rise or maybe he just wants the peace of mind that comes from paying off debts).

Peter's pension income will now be:

£110,877 x 7% less 20% tax = £6,209

We'll also assume that Ian withdraws £36,959 from his £88,702 ISA fund to pay off his mortgage. Ian's income on his remaining ISA savings will now be:

£51,743 x 7% less 0% tax = £3,622

Peter the pension saver now has 71% more retirement income than Ian the ISA investor!

The difference comes about because Ian has to use proportionately more of his ISA savings to pay off his mortgage.

In summary, the above case study reveals that if you go from being a higher-rate taxpayer to a basic-rate taxpayer when you retire, you will end up with significantly more income from a pension than an ISA.

The Income Tax Personal Allowance

In the above example I assumed that Peter paid 20% income tax on all of his pension income. The implicit assumption was that his income tax personal allowance was used up by other taxable income, perhaps his state pension and income from rental properties or a part-time job or part-time business he has to keep himself busy.

I taxed all of his private pension income because I did not want to overstate the benefits of pension saving. In reality, some of the income you receive from a private pension plan may be tax free thanks to your income tax personal allowance.

The standard income tax personal allowance for the current 2014/15 tax year is £10,000 and will increase to £10,500 next year.

There are additional age-related allowances but these are being phased out and are no longer available to those turning 65. Nevertheless, the sharp increase in the standard income tax personal allowance in recent years means that most retirees will continue to receive a significant proportion of their income tax free.

Once you reach state pension age your state pension will probably use up most of your personal allowance. However, you can start withdrawing money from your other pensions up to 10 years earlier. If during this period your taxable income from other sources (e.g. rental property) does not use up all of your personal allowance, some of your pension withdrawals will be tax free.

If some of your pension income is tax-free this will make pensions even more attractive retirement saving vehicles than ISAs.

Chapter 13

ISAs vs Pensions:
Inheritance Tax Planning

Your Spouse

When you die your ISAs will form part of your estate for inheritance tax purposes (although certain AIM shares are exempt after two years). There is no inheritance tax on assets, including ISAs, left to your spouse.

However, it's critical to point out that the money will no longer be allowed to stay in an ISA wrapper – in other words, it will no longer be tax free!

As a result, your spouse's after-tax income could fall significantly when you die.

Your spouse will be able to put the money back into his or her own ISA. With an annual investment limit of £15,000, this could take just a short amount of time or many years, depending on the amount of money involved.

With pensions, if your savings are in an income drawdown arrangement, the fund can be used to continue paying a pension to your spouse. The investments in the fund will continue to grow tax free.

Your Children

Pension savings left to your adult children when you die or after your spouse dies will generally be subject to a recovery tax (currently 55%), often with no additional inheritance tax.

The recovery tax is not payable if you die before the age of 75 and before you have started withdrawing money from your pension.

ISA savings will be subject to inheritance tax but only if the assets in the estate are over the threshold – currently £325,000 but up to £650,000 for married couples.

Although 55% is higher than the 40% inheritance tax rate, we know from the case study in the previous chapter that, thanks to the initial income tax relief, a pension pot could contain a lot more money than an ISA.

If your ISA savings are subject to 40% inheritance tax it is possible that your children will receive a much bigger lump sum payout from your pension, despite the recovery tax charge. If your ISA savings are not subject to inheritance tax, however, your children will possibly receive a bigger payout from your ISAs.

It is impossible to provide a definitive answer to this question at present because the Government believes that the flat 55% recovery tax is too high. It may be reduced from April 2015 but to what extent has not been revealed.

Are ISAs Still a Good Investment?

In Chapter 12 it was shown that pensions are usually a much better tax shelter than ISAs. However, there are 17 million ISA savers in Britain and I'm one of them!

What attracts so many people to ISAs is their flexibility. You can withdraw money at any time. Pension investors have to wait until they reach the minimum retirement age of 55 or older.

As with everything in life, a compromise is usually the best solution. There's no harm in using both.

And as we will see in the next two chapters, an ISA is a great place to park money **before** you invest it in a pension.

Part 4

Postponing & Accelerating Pension Saving

Chapter 14

Basic-Rate Taxpayers: Should They Make Pension Contributions?

Financial advisors usually advise people to start making pension contributions as early as possible. They usually point to the 'magic' of compound interest. Compound interest – earning interest on interest – seems to possess magical powers, making millionaires out of just about anyone who starts early enough.

However, what I think financial advisors often get confused about is saving in a pension with saving *generally*. It's never too early to start saving... but it may be too early to start saving in a pension.

In previous chapters I have shown that higher-rate taxpayers enjoy twice as much tax relief on their pension contributions as basic-rate taxpayers. A higher-rate taxpayer is someone who has taxable income of more than £41,865 in the 2014/15 tax year.

So the question is, should you delay making pension contributions if you are currently a basic-rate taxpayer but expect to become a higher-rate taxpayer in the future?

More specifically, should you invest your savings somewhere else, for example in a tax-free ISA, and transfer the money into a pension when you will enjoy much more income tax relief?

This is the question we will answer in this chapter.

Are You a Temporary Basic-Rate Taxpayer?

There are lots of reasons why an individual may be a basic-rate taxpayer in one tax year but a higher-rate taxpayer in another tax year.

The most obvious reason is career progression: a graduate earns a lot less income than someone with the same qualifications and

20 years' work experience. You may start your working life as a basic-rate taxpayer and become a higher-rate taxpayer a number of years later.

Many self-employed business owners who are normally higher-rate taxpayers may be basic-rate taxpayers from time to time, either because their incomes fall during tough economic conditions or because they have abnormally high tax-deductible expenditure during any given tax year, for example if they make significant investments in equipment.

Many company directors are also basic-rate taxpayers in some years but higher-rate taxpayers in other years, for example if they pay themselves a small dividend during one tax year and a big dividend during another tax year.

Wealth Warning

There is one group of individuals who should always consider making pension contributions, even if they are only temporary basic-rate taxpayers: company employees who belong to generous workplace pension schemes. For them tax relief is only one of the benefits of making pension contributions. The employer will often match, or more than match, the contribution made by the employee – effectively handing over free cash which no thrifty person would turn down (more on this in Chapter 19).

Case Study – Postponing Pension Contributions

Penny and Isabella are both basic-rate taxpayers but expect to be higher-rate taxpayers in three years' time. Both want to save £3,000 per year but they have different strategies. Penny decides to put her savings in a personal pension straight away because her father has advised her to start saving for retirement as soon as possible. Isabella also wants to save for her retirement but she also wants to maximise her tax relief. She decides to invest in an ISA until she is a higher-rate taxpayer and then transfer the money into a pension.

Who ends up better off?

Table 3
Pension vs ISA
Temporary Basic-Rate Taxpayers

End Year	Pension £	ISA £
1	4,013	3,210
2	8,306	6,645
3	12,900	10,320

We'll assume they both enjoy investment returns of 7% per year (tax-free inside both an ISA and pension). Penny's £3,000 annual investment is topped up with £750 of free cash from the taxman so her gross pension contribution is £3,750. After a year this will have grown to £4,013. After three years she will have £12,900.

Isabella's £3,000 ISA investment will be worth £3,210 after one year. After three years she will have £10,320. The results are summarised in Table 3. For every £1 Penny has in her pension, Isabella has just 80p – the difference is down to the 20% basic-rate tax relief Penny enjoys on her pension contributions.

Becoming Higher-rate Taxpayers

It's the start of the fourth tax year and Isabella knows she will be a higher-rate taxpayer this year. So she decides to take her £10,320 ISA savings and stick them into her newly opened pension plan. The taxman will add £2,580 in basic-rate tax relief and, hey presto, she has £12,900 sitting in her pension plan, just like Penny.

However, as a higher-rate taxpayer, Isabella will also receive higher-rate tax relief when she submits her tax return. To calculate this we simply multiply her gross pension contribution by 20%:

£12,900 x 20% = £2,580

In summary, Penny and Isabella have both saved exactly the same amount of money but because Isabella waited until she became a higher-rate taxpayer before making pension contributions she ends up with £2,580 more than Penny.

Maximising the Pension Pot

In the above example Isabella has the same amount of money as Penny in her pension plus a tax refund from HMRC. However, if Isabella would prefer to maximise her pension savings she could do things slightly differently.

What she could do is make a bigger pension contribution – £13,760 instead of just her £10,320 ISA savings. The taxman will top this up with £3,440 to produce a gross pension contribution of £17,200. Isabella won't be out of pocket despite making a bigger contribution because she will also receive a tax refund of £3,440 (£17,200 x 20%) – her higher-rate relief.

This means her total personal investment will simply be the amount she saved up in her ISA:

£13,760 pension contribution *minus* £3,440 tax refund = £10,320

Now look at the size of Isabella's pension pot. She has £17,200 compared with Penny's £12,900 – 33% more money!

33% – The Magic Number

The same 33% increase in pension savings can be enjoyed by anyone who postpones making pension contributions while temporarily a basic-rate taxpayer.

Regardless of whether you postpone for one year, 10 years or any other time period, and regardless of whether you are making big or small pension contributions, the result is exactly the same:

Your pension pot will be 33% bigger

It's a bit like buying a bottle of fine wine and storing it away, instead of drinking it immediately. Good things come to those who wait.

Finally, remember that, although Isabella postpones her pension contributions, she does NOT postpone saving. Note too that she invests in an ISA so that, like Penny, she does not miss out on tax-free growth.

Practical Pointers

- The assumption is that Isabella enjoys the maximum higher-rate tax relief on her £17,200 pension contribution. However, we know from Chapter 3 that Isabella will only enjoy full higher-rate tax relief if she also has at least £17,200 of income taxed at 40%. If she doesn't, she may have to spread her pension contributions over more than one tax year.

- Isabella personally contributes £13,760, which is more than her £10,320 ISA savings. However, when she gets her tax refund back she is not left out of pocket. How do we calculate the number £13,760? Simply divide £10,320 by 0.75 to add on the higher-rate tax relief.

Chapter 15

Higher-Rate Taxpayers: Can They Put Off Pension Saving?

In the previous chapter I showed how basic-rate taxpayers may be better off postponing pension contributions until they become higher-rate taxpayers. What about higher-rate taxpayers – can they also put off making pension contributions?

Be careful about asking a financial advisor this question by the way. It's like giving Superman Kryptonite. They usually advise people to start making pension contributions as soon as possible. However, as I pointed out in the previous chapter, they often confuse the benefits of saving in a pension with the benefits of saving *generally*.

There are lots of reasons why you might not feel like putting money into a pension right now, even though you would receive lots of tax relief. It all revolves around the lengthy jail sentence placed on pension savings – you can't access them until you are age 55 or older.

If you have big financial commitments, for example a mortgage or children's education to pay for many years, you may be very reluctant to tie up your savings in a pension.

You certainly shouldn't be making any pension contributions if you are in imminent danger of losing a big chunk or all of your income, for example if your business is struggling or you are worried about losing your job.

Am I saying it's not necessary to save in these situations? No, I'm a big fan of saving from day one. What I am saying is that you don't necessarily have to save via a pension... not at certain stages of your life at least. It's a fat lot of good having £100,000 in your pension pot if your home's about to be repossessed.

Before making any pension contributions, you should always make sure you have a significant amount of money saved elsewhere to protect against:

- An unforeseen drop in income, and
- Unforeseen expenses

But what about all the tax savings enjoyed by pension savers? If you delay putting money into a pension, won't you lose out? This is one of the great misconceptions about pensions.

As it happens, if you want immediate access to your savings, you don't have to put money into a pension until you are ready.

You will not be one penny worse off than someone who makes pension contributions continually for many years.

I've never heard any pension experts make this crucial point. Maybe it's because advising people to put off making pension contributions is bad for business, a bit like a tobacco company telling you to quit smoking.

Case Study – Postponing Pension Contributions

In Chapter 12 we compared Peter the pension saver with Ian the ISA investor. What we discovered is that pensions are much more powerful than ISAs – you could end up with at least 40% more income from a pension.

However, it is possible that Ian, the ISA investor, will have the last laugh. Let's say he originally started saving into an ISA because he wanted access to his savings. Back then he was worried about losing his job and also had a big mortgage and three children to support. Move forward five years, his career's going well, the mortgage is much smaller and the children all have their own jobs.

So he decides to take his ISA savings and stick them into a pension. Is he still worse off than Peter, who started saving in a pension five years earlier?

Table 4
Postponing Pension Contributions
Higher-Rate Taxpayers

End Year	Pension £	ISA £
1	10,700	6,420
2	22,149	13,289
3	34,399	20,640
4	47,507	28,504
5	61,533	36,920

Peter and Ian's savings up to the end of year five are summarised in Table 4. Just to recap, both are higher-rate taxpayers and both personally invest £6,000 per year. Peter enjoys income tax relief so his gross pension contribution is £10,000 per year, compared with Ian's £6,000 ISA investment. They both enjoy tax-free growth of 7% per year. After one year their £10,000 and £6,000 initial investments will be worth £10,700 and £6,420 respectively (explaining the first numbers you see in the table).

After five years Peter has £61,533, compared with Ian's £36,920. Ian now takes his ISA savings and sticks them in a pension. Because he knows he'll get a tax refund (his higher-rate tax relief) he actually makes an investment of £49,226 (£36,920/0.75). The taxman adds £12,307 of basic-rate tax relief and, hey presto, Ian ends up with £61,533 sitting in his pension pot – exactly the same as Peter!

Ian also gets a tax refund of £12,307 (£61,533 x 20%), so his £49,226 pension investment costs him just £36,920 personally – exactly the amount he accumulated in ISAs.

In summary, Peter started saving in a pension from day one, whereas Ian put his savings into an ISA, before transferring the money into a pension five years later. By postponing his pension contributions, Ian was able to access his savings in the event of a financial emergency. Postponing his contributions has not left him out of pocket.

Postponing Pension Contributions – The Dangers

I'm not encouraging anyone to postpone making pension contributions. The point of this exercise is to show that, all things being equal, there is *mathematically* no difference between regular pension contributions and a big catch-up pension contribution. Saving in a pension over many years will not leave you better off.

As with everything, compromise is often the best solution. There's nothing to stop you making some pension contributions now and further catch-up contributions when your personal financial situation is healthier.

There are also some dangers and some very important practical issues when it comes to postponing pension contributions:

Danger # 1 Higher Rate Tax Relief Could Be Scrapped

We discussed this danger in Chapter 5. You cannot trust politicians not to meddle or break promises. In recent times some politicians have proposed scrapping higher-rate tax relief on pension contributions, leaving just basic-rate tax relief (the taxman's top up).

For this reason some pension experts advise higher-rate taxpayers to make pension contributions NOW, in other words to make hay while the sun shines.

If there is no higher-rate tax relief when Ian makes his catch-up pension contribution in five years' time, he will end up with just £46,150 in his pension pot (£36,920/0.8) – over £15,000 less than Peter.

Danger # 2 Loss of Employer Pension Contributions

If you belong to a workplace pension scheme and your employer is matching the contributions you make personally, postponing contributions could prove costly: you will lose a lot of free cash being offered by your employer (see Chapter 19).

Danger # 3 Your Earnings Fall

If your income falls and you are no longer a higher-rate taxpayer when the time comes to make catch-up contributions, you will not enjoy any higher-rate tax relief.

This could happen if you own a business that enters a long tough patch or period of decline. It could also happen to a company employee who suffers redundancy and is unable to find another job that pays well.

There are also practical issues when it comes to postponing pension contributions:

Practical Issue # 1 Maximising Higher Rate Tax Relief

Ian has to make a gross pension contribution of £61,533 to catch up with Peter. We know from Chapter 3 that to obtain the maximum higher-rate tax relief he must also have at least £61,533 of income taxed at 40%. Most people don't.

The bigger your catch-up contribution, the less likely you are to obtain the maximum higher-rate tax relief.

Fortunately, there is a solution to this problem: Ian could spread his catch-up contributions over several tax years so that his higher-rate tax relief is maximised.

This means he shouldn't leave it too close to retirement to make his catch-up contributions, especially if he has additional savings that he would like to put into a pension, in addition to his ISA savings.

Practical Issue # 2 Exceeding the Annual Allowance

The bigger your catch-up contribution, the more likely you are to exceed the annual allowance (see Chapter 2). The annual allowance was reduced from £50,000 to £40,000 at the start of the 2014/15 tax year and could be reduced further in the years ahead.

Fortunately, it is possible to carry forward any unused annual allowance from the three previous tax years, so a gross pension contribution of up to £190,000 is allowed in 2014/15, provided you have sufficient relevant UK earnings and belonged to a pension scheme in each of those years.

Again, the best practical solution for Ian would probably be to spread his contributions over several tax years.

Practical Issue # 3 Tax Free Growth

An important reason why Ian is able to catch up with Peter is because he also enjoys tax-free investment growth by putting his money in an ISA. If Ian's savings are taxed, he will end up permanently worse off, even after he puts his savings in a pension.

In summary, it is possible to put off pension saving if you don't want to tie up your money right now... but there are some dangers and practical obstacles.

Chapter 16

How to Protect Your Child Benefit

Child benefit is an extremely valuable tax-free gift from the Government to parents. Those who qualify currently receive the following annual payments:

- £1,066 for the first child
- £704.60 for each subsequent child

Depending on the number of children, a family can expect to receive the following total child benefit payment:

Children	Total Child Benefit
1	£1,066
2	£1,771
3	£2,475
4	£3,180

plus £704.60 for each additional child

You can keep receiving child benefit until your children are 16 years of age or until age 20 if they are enrolled in 'relevant education' (the likes of GCSEs, A Levels, and NVQs to level 3, but not degree courses).

That's the good news. The bad news is the Government withdraws the benefit where any member of the household has annual income in excess of £50,000.

The withdrawal operates by levying an income tax charge on the highest earner in the household.

How the Child Benefit Charge Works

For every £100 the highest earner's income exceeds £50,000, there is a tax charge equivalent to 1% of the child benefit. So if the highest earner in the household has an income of £51,000, the tax charge is 10% of the child benefit.

For a household with two children this means a tax charge of £177 (£1,771 x 10%, rounded down to the nearest whole pound).

If the highest earner has an income of £55,000, the tax charge is 50% of the child benefit. For a household with two children this means a tax charge of £885.

Once the highest earner's income reaches £60,000, all the child benefit will effectively have been withdrawn.

As an alternative to the income tax charge, the claimant can choose not to receive child benefit.

1970s Style Tax Rates

The child benefit charge creates some truly eye-watering marginal tax rates for some parents with income between £50,000 and £60,000.

For example, let's say the highest earner's taxable income goes up from £50,000 to £51,000 in 2014/15.

They will pay £400 more income tax and a 10% child benefit charge – £106 for a household with one child. So the total tax charge on the additional £1,000 is £506 – that's a marginal tax rate of 51%!

And if you think that's bad, take a look at the marginal tax rates suffered by parents with more than one child:

2 Children	58%
3 Children	65%
4 Children	72%

You can add an extra 2% to all of the above tax rates to take account of national insurance, if your income is from employment or self-employment. The marginal tax rates for dividends are different.

Not all Income is Equal

The child benefit charge only applies if your 'adjusted net income' is over £50,000. Adjusted net income includes all income subject to income tax, including income from employment, profits from self employment, pensions and income from property, savings and dividends.

Income from tax-free investments like ISAs is excluded. What this means is that a parent with work-related income of £50,000 and tax-free dividends of £10,000 from an ISA will avoid the child benefit charge completely; someone with the same £50,000 of earned income but £10,000 of rental income will effectively lose all of their child benefit.

This makes investments like shares and bonds (that can be sheltered inside an ISA) potentially far more tax efficient than rental property.

For example, that £10,000 in rental income will produce an income tax bill of £4,000 and a child benefit charge of £1,771 for a family with two children. Total rental income net of all taxes is just £4,229.

The ISA investor ends up with 136% more income!

How Pension Contributions Can Help You Avoid the Child Benefit Charge

One of the simplest ways for almost all taxpayers to avoid the child benefit charge is by making pension contributions. Your adjusted net income is reduced by your gross pension contributions.

In Chapter 15 we looked at the pros and cons of postponing pension contributions. However, those with income in the £50,000-£60,000 bracket are a special case. They should be very wary of postponing making pension contributions if they are subject to the child benefit charge.

In fact, people in this income group should consider *bringing forward* their pension contributions, i.e. making bigger contributions now and smaller ones when their incomes rise above £60,000.

The key tax planning point is that you shouldn't necessarily think in terms of avoiding the child benefit charge completely or permanently. It may be possible for some taxpayers (especially those earning just over £50,000) to achieve this best case scenario. For those with income close to £60,000 (or over £60,000 in some cases) it may be more practical to think in terms of reducing only part of the charge or reducing the charge in some tax years but not others.

Let's take a look at some of the potential tax savings:

Example
Alan has taxable income of £55,000 in 2014/15. His wife earns £30,000 and claims child benefit for three children: £2,475. On the top £5,000 slice of his income, Alan faces a £2,000 income tax bill and a child benefit charge of £1,237 (50%). Alan's £5,000 is reduced to just £1,763.

Let's focus in on that top £5,000 slice of his income and see how he can protect himself from the child benefit charge:

Alan personally contributes £4,000 into his pension. The taxman adds £1,000 of basic-rate tax relief, producing a gross pension contribution of £5,000. When Alan submits his tax return he also receives £1,000 of higher-rate tax relief (£5,000 x 20%).

Furthermore, because Alan's adjusted net income has fallen to £50,000, he escapes the £1,237 child benefit charge.

Alan enjoys a total of £3,237 tax relief on his £5,000 pension contribution, i.e. 65% tax relief.

He ends up with £5,000 in his pension pot instead of £1,763 in after-tax income.

What this example shows is that many parents in the £50,000-£60,000 bracket will enjoy tax relief on their pension contributions of 58% (two children), 65% (three children) or maybe even more, compared with the 40% tax relief enjoyed by most other higher-rate taxpayers.

Hence it's not just basic-rate taxpayers who should consider postponing pension contributions until their incomes rise (see Chapter 14). Higher-rate taxpayers with income over £41,865 but under £50,000 may wish to consider postponing pension contributions if they expect to be in the £50,000-£60,000 income bracket in the near future and subject to the child benefit charge.

Similarly, where one spouse or partner is in the £50,000-£60,000 income bracket, and the other has a smaller income, it may be worth getting the higher earner to make all the family's pension contributions, even for just one or two tax years.

Example
Chris and Maria are both higher-rate taxpayers earning £60,000 and £50,000 respectively. They receive child benefit for two children: £1,771. In the past they've each made pension contributions of £5,000.

In 2014/15 the couple decide that Maria should stop her pension contributions and Chris should increase his by £5,000 to £10,000. By making an additional £5,000 pension contribution Chris will avoid an additional 50% child benefit charge, saving the couple £885.

Bigger than Normal Pension Contributions

Those in the £50,000-£60,000 income bracket should consider making bigger than normal pension contributions, in particular if they expect their income to rise above £60,000 in the future or if their children are approaching the age where child benefit will be withdrawn.

Example
Gordon has taxable income of £60,000 in 2014/15. His wife earns £30,000 and claims child benefit for two children: £1,771. On the top £10,000 slice of his income, Gordon faces a 58% tax charge: £4,000 income tax and a £1,771 child benefit charge.

Gordon wouldn't normally make a gross pension contribution of more than £5,000 but decides to double his contribution for the current tax year so that he can take advantage of the 58% tax relief available (two children).

He could then suspend making any pension contributions in 2015/16, for example if his income rises from £60,000 to £65,000. A £5,000 pension contribution in 2015/16 would attract just 40% tax relief, compared with the 58% available in 2014/15.

Much Bigger than Normal Pension Contributions

Even those with income *over* £60,000 can enjoy above average levels of tax relief by making bigger than normal pension contributions.

Example
Colin has taxable income of £65,000 in 2014/15. His wife earns £30,000 and receives child benefit for three children: £2,475. On the top £15,000 slice of his income, Colin faces an £8,475 tax charge: £6,000 income tax and a £2,475 child benefit charge.

If Colin makes a gross pension contribution of £5,000 he will enjoy 40% tax relief, just like most other higher-rate taxpayers. He will not avoid any of the child benefit charge because his adjusted net income will not fall below £60,000.

Fortunately his aunt Doris left him some money in her will so Colin decides to make a much bigger than normal £15,000 gross pension contribution in 2014/15 and then stop making contributions for a year or two.

Colin's pension contribution attracts £6,000 income tax relief and, by reducing his adjusted net income to £50,000, allows him to entirely avoid the £2,475 child benefit charge. The total tax relief is £8,475 or 57% of his gross pension contribution.

Obviously the higher your income the bigger the pension contribution you have to make to get your income below £60,000 and ultimately down to £50,000. However, for some individuals, including those with income well over £60,000, the tax relief may make it worthwhile

The Self-Employed

The taxable income of self-employed individuals (sole traders etc) tends to fluctuate more than that of salaried employees and even company owners.

A self-employed individual's taxable income is essentially the pre-tax profits of the business. These will vary from year to year if business conditions improve or decline or if the business owner alters the level of tax deductible spending (e.g. by making investments in tax deductible equipment or vehicles).

As a result some self-employed business owners, who are also parents of qualifying children, may find themselves in the £50,000-£60,000 income bracket in some tax years but not others.

Where possible they should consider always making pension contribution in those '£50,000-£60,000' tax years, possibly contributions that are bigger than normal.

Both Partners Earn £50,000-£60,000

Where both income earners in the household are in the £50,000-£60,000 bracket, the most tax-efficient strategy is to *equalise* their adjusted net incomes.

Example
Alistair earns £58,000, his wife Wilma earns £55,000. The couple want to make a £5,000 gross pension contribution in 2014/15. If Alistair makes the entire contribution this will take his adjusted net income to £53,000. Wilma will then become the household's highest earner with £55,000, resulting in a 50% child benefit charge.

The best solution may be for Alistair to make a £4,000 gross pension contribution, with Wilma making a £1,000 gross contribution. They will both then have adjusted net income of £54,000 and an additional 10% of their child benefit will be retained.

Other Considerations & Drawbacks

To maximise the tax relief on pension contributions it may be necessary to postpone or bring forward contributions or have one household member make bigger contributions than another.

Actions like these may have other consequences that need to be considered. For example, the second member of the household may not be happy about the highest earner accumulating all the retirement savings!

Postponing pension contributions may not be a good idea if this means you forfeit contributions from your employer (see Chapter 19) or if higher-rate tax relief is eventually abolished (see Chapter 5).

Chapter 17

Higher Income Earners

There are three groups of individuals who should consider making pension contributions sooner rather than later:

- Those with income between £100,000 and £120,000
- Those with income over £120,000
- Those with income over £150,000

Income between £100,000 and £120,000

Once your income exceeds £100,000 your income tax personal allowance is gradually taken away. It is reduced by £1 for every £2 you earn above £100,000.

For example, if your income is £110,000 your personal allowance will be reduced by £5,000.

The income tax personal allowance for the 2014/15 tax year is £10,000. So once your income reaches £120,000 you will have no personal allowance at all.

This is a real tax sting for those earning over £100,000. The personal allowance saves you £4,000 in tax if you are a higher-rate taxpayer.

Paying Tax at 60%

The effect of having your personal allowance taken away is that anyone earning between £100,000 and £120,000 faces a hefty marginal income tax rate of 60%.

For example, someone who earns £100,000 and receives an extra £10,000 will pay 40% tax on the extra income – £4,000. They'll also have their personal allowance reduced by £5,000, which means they'll have to pay an extra £2,000 in tax (£5,000 x 40%). Total tax on extra income: £6,000 which is 60%!

Saving Tax at 60%

The flipside of this is that anyone in this income bracket who makes pension contributions will enjoy 60% tax relief.

Your personal allowance is reduced if your 'adjusted net income' is more than £100,000. When calculating your adjusted net income you usually deduct any pension contributions you have made.

For example, let's say you have taxable income of £110,000 and invest £8,000 in a pension. For starters you will receive a £2,000 top up from the taxman (your basic-rate tax relief), resulting in a gross pension contribution of £10,000. You'll also receive higher-rate tax relief of £2,000 (£10,000 x 20%).

In addition, by making a gross pension of £10,000 your 'adjusted net income' will be reduced from £110,000 to £100,000, so none of your personal allowance will be taken away. Additional tax saving: £2,000 (£5,000 x 40%).

In summary, your £10,000 pension contribution produces £6,000 of tax savings – a total of 60% tax relief!

Income over £120,000

Once your income rises above £120,000 your marginal income tax rate falls back to 40%. However, making quite big pension contributions can still be attractive because you may still get 60% tax relief on some of the money you put away.

For example, let's say you have taxable income of £125,000 and put £20,000 into a pension. Like anyone else you will receive £5,000 basic-rate tax relief, resulting in a gross pension contribution of £25,000. And like any other higher-rate taxpayer you will receive an additional £5,000 of higher-rate relief (£25,000 x 20%).

In addition, your £25,000 gross pension contribution will reduce your adjusted net income from £125,000 to £100,000, so none of your personal allowance will be taken away. Additional tax saving: £4,000 (£10,000 x 40%).

In summary, your £25,000 gross pension contribution produces £14,000 of tax savings – a total of 56% tax relief!

In fact, anyone with taxable income of up to £140,000 will enjoy *at least* 50% tax relief by making a gross pension contribution that's big enough to take their adjusted net income back down to £100,000.

For example, someone with taxable income of £140,000 would need to make a gross pension contribution of £40,000 to take their adjusted net income back down to £100,000 and enjoy exactly 50% tax relief.

Although the tax relief is attractive, that's a big pension contribution, so in practice this strategy may appeal most to those whose income is only slightly higher than the £120,000 threshold.

Income over £150,000

Once your income rises above £150,000 you start paying income tax at 45% on most types of income. The flipside of this is that, by making pension contributions, you can enjoy 45% tax relief.

Example
Jennifer has taxable income of £175,000. As things stand she will pay 45% tax on £25,000 of her income. If she puts £20,000 into her pension she will receive £5,000 of basic-rate tax relief, resulting in a gross pension contribution of £25,000.

Her basic-rate band will also be increased by £25,000 which means £25,000 of her income will be taxed at 20% instead of 45%, saving her an additional £6,250 in income tax.

Total tax relief: £11,250 (£5,000 + £6,250), which is 45% of her gross pension contribution.

Will 45% become 40%?

A key question for high income earners is: Will the top rate of income tax be reduced from 45% back to 40% and, if so, when? When the reduction from 50% to 45% was announced in the 2012 Budget, no date was given for a further cut to 40%.

The Liberal Democrats have fiercely resisted calls from Conservative backbenchers to reduce the top rate further. Earlier this year, Chief Secretary to the Treasury Danny Alexander claimed that any further cut would only happen "over my dead body" while the party was in government.

Reducing taxes on high income earners will continue to be very difficult politically while those on lower incomes are suffering from pay freezes and cuts in tax allowances and benefits (e.g. the withdrawal of child benefit from middle-income households).

If anything, the top tax rate could be increased back to 50%. Labour has pledged to do this if they win the next election. However, this does NOT mean you should postpone making pension contributions so that you can obtain 50% tax relief instead of 45% tax relief (see below).

Tax Relief for High Earners

Another important issue for high income earners is whether the tax relief on their pension contributions will be restricted in some way in the future.

This seems extremely likely if there is a change of government. As part of its next election manifesto, the Labour Party has also pledged to restrict pension tax relief for people earning over £150,000 to the same rate as basic-rate taxpayers.

If you think a change of government is a distinct possibility, you should consider making bigger than normal contributions with full tax relief while you can.

Part 5

Employees

Chapter 18

Auto-Enrolment: The Advent of Compulsory Pensions

"Currently 14 million people get no contribution from their employer towards a pension."

Former Secretary of State for Work and Pension, Yvette Cooper, January 2010.

If your employer currently does not make pension contributions for you, you will be interested to know about the new system of compulsory pensions coming into existence over the next few years.

Known as 'auto enrolment' it forces all employers to enrol nearly all their staff into a pension between October 2012 and February 2018.

A state-sponsored pension scheme called NEST (National Employment Savings Trust) is being made available to employers, who do not have their own pension scheme.

The Pensions Regulator will write to employers to tell them their precise 'staging date', 12 months in advance.

Of course, many of the biggest employers already offer a pension. It's the smallest businesses that are least likely to have one in place.

The auto-enrolment staging dates for small firms vary considerably from now until 2018.

If you want to find out your employer's precise staging date, you can do so by entering its PAYE reference number (found on your annual P60) into the following online calculator:

www.thepensionsregulator.gov.uk/employers/tools/staging-date.aspx

Exemptions

Employees exempt from auto enrolment include those:

- Earning below the 'earnings trigger' (£10,000 in 2014/15)
- Under 22 years of age
- Over state pension age
- Company directors not considered to be 'employed' or the only worker in the business
- Already in a qualifying pension scheme

Certain groups of employees do not need to be auto-enrolled but must be given the right to opt in if they want, including those:

- Over 16 and under 22
- Over state pension age and under 75
- With earnings between the lower earnings limit and the earnings trigger (£5,772-£10,000 for 2014/15)

The Contributions

Employers will be forced to make a minimum pension contribution and, in practice, so too will most employees.

Contributions will be a percentage of 'qualifying earnings'. The minimum contribution will be increased gradually until October 2018.

Contributions will start at 2% with at least 1% coming from the employer. From October 2018 onwards the total minimum contribution will be 8%, with at least 3% coming from the employer.

The minimum contributions are summarised in Table 5.

Table 5
Auto-Enrolment: Minimum Contributions

	Employer pays	Total required	Employee could pay
Employer's staging date to September 2017	1%	2%	1%
1 October 2017 to 30 September 2018	2%	5%	3%
From 1 October 2018	3%	8%	5%

The total minimum contribution can be paid by the employer but in practice many small firms will probably insist that the employee makes up the required balance.

This means that from October 2018 onwards many employees will be forced to contribute 5% to a pension if they want to benefit from a 3% contribution from their employer.

Employees' contributions will enjoy tax relief as normal, which means 4% will come from them personally and the extra 1% will be added by the taxman in the form of basic-rate tax relief.

Qualifying Earnings

The minimum contributions are not based on the employee's total earnings but rather on a band of earnings.

The lower and upper thresholds for 2014/15 are £5,772 and £41,865 respectively. What this means is that compulsory pension contributions are based on earnings of up to £36,093 (£41,865 - £5,772).

For example, someone with employment income of £50,000 will have their compulsory pension contributions based on earnings of £36,093. Someone with employment income of £20,000 will have their compulsory pension contributions based on earnings of £14,228 (£20,000 - £5,772).

Opting out

Employees will be automatically enrolled but can opt out if they wish by completing an opt-out notice. Every three years the employer will have to re-enrol those who have opted out.

No doubt many employees, especially younger employees, will prefer to opt out if they are compelled by their employers to make a pension contribution of up to 5%.

How Valuable is Auto Enrolment?

The answer to this question probably depends on whether you are an employee or employer.

Many small business owners cannot afford to save for their own retirement, let alone those of their entire workforce!

And this, perhaps, is the crucial point. If your employer is dragged kicking and screaming into a system of compulsory pensions, you may end up being paid less to cover the cost. For example, future pay increases or other employment benefits may be reduced. This is basic economics.

Another problem for many employees is that they will only receive the 3% employer contribution from October 2018 onwards. That's over four years away!

Even a 3% employer contribution is not big enough to solve anyone's retirement saving problem, especially since it will only be based on a small band of the employee's earnings.

For example, let's say you currently earn £40,000 and your employer makes a 3% pension contribution for 20 years (based on the £36,093 band of qualifying earnings), with all amounts increased to take account of inflation.

After 20 years the employer contributions will be worth around £60,000, if the investments in the fund grow by 7% per year. That's a tidy little sum BUT insignificant in terms of providing you with a meaningful retirement income.

In 20 years' time your salary will have grown to around £70,000, so the money paid into your pension pot by your employer will be worth less than one year's salary.

If that money is used to buy an annuity or some other type of scheme pension, the annual income may be around £3,500, which is around 5% of your final salary. It's not really enough for a golden retirement!

Chapter 19

Free Cash from Employers

Many individuals enjoy more than just tax relief on their pension contributions. They also receive free money from their employers.

By signing up to the workplace pension scheme, they may receive employer contributions totalling 5%-10% of their salary, provided they contribute a similar amount.

With the help of employer pension contributions, you may be able to save twice as quickly as you could on your own. Sometimes employers will double what you put in. For example, in one pension scheme I know about, the company puts in 12% if the employee puts in 6%.

Many employees recognize that giving up any of this free money (by not contributing at all or not contributing enough) is tantamount to looking a gift horse in the mouth.

I remember listening on the radio to a very eloquent married woman describe how she and her husband were trying to cut out every single bit of frivolous spending so that they could contribute as much as possible to her husband's workplace pension scheme, thereby enjoying a hefty matching contribution from his employer.

She described it as "austerity today for prosperity tomorrow".

However, not everyone is as financially prudent as this couple. According to Standard Life, in 2011 employers were offering a contribution to around 10 million employees but around 4.5 million did not sign up to their employer's pension scheme.

These employees were missing out on a total of nearly £6 billion per year of free money!

Not surprisingly it is younger employees who contribute the least to pensions. According to the Department for Work and Pensions, in 2011 only 15% of employees aged 16-24 participated in workplace pension schemes, whereas pension participation was 58% in the 45-54 age group.

Membership is increasing with the introduction of compulsory pensions (see Chapter 18) BUT this will take many years to roll out and many employees (e.g. younger employees) may opt out.

I'm not in the business of criticising the savings habits of others, especially those who have children to support. Many families have very little income left after paying extortionate amounts of income tax, national insurance and VAT and after paying down debts like student loans and home mortgages.

Nevertheless, if there is ever a good time to contribute to a pension it's when your employer is offering you money on a plate.

Example

Douglas is an employee with a salary of £50,000 a year. Let's say his employer offers to make a 5% pension contribution if Douglas also contributes 5% personally.

If Douglas decides <u>not</u> to join his workplace pension scheme, he will have an additional £2,500 of disposable income (£50,000 x 5%). After paying income tax he will be left with £1,500.

Alternatively, if Douglas decides to join his workplace pension scheme he will end up with £5,000 sitting in his pension (£2,500 contributed personally and £2,500 from his employer).

Douglas has to decide whether £1,500 of income today is more valuable than £5,000 tucked away until he retires.

This is just a snapshot from a single year. Douglas will lose £3,500 (£5,000 - £1,500) every year he is not a member of his employer's pension scheme.

Furthermore, he will also lose the tax-free growth on that money. If a 25-year-old decides to forego a pension contribution from his employer he will lose possibly 40 years of tax-free compound growth. On next year's foregone contribution he will lose 39 years of tax-free growth... and so on.

So how much do you stand to lose over the long term by not receiving pension contributions from your employer?

Example continued

Let's say Douglas does not belong to his workplace pension scheme for five years and therefore loses out on five years of employer contributions (at 5% of his salary).

We'll assume his salary increases by 3% per year (to compensate for inflation), which means the contributions from his employer will also grow by 3% per year. We'll also assume the money in his pension grows by 7% per year tax free.

Douglas loses out on the following employer contributions over the five-year period: £2,500, £2,575, £2,652, £2,732 and £2,814. When you add tax-free compound growth at 7% per year, the total value of the employer pension contributions after five years is £16,269.

However, that's not the end of the story. Depending on how far away Douglas is from retirement he could lose out on tax-free growth on this money for possibly another 10, 20, 30 or even 40 years. For example, those five years' worth of contributions will be worth £22,818 after 10 years, £44,887 after 20 years, £88,300 after 30 years and £173,699 after 40 years.

Remember, all we are looking at here are the contributions that would be made by Douglas's employer (the 'free money'). We are ignoring the contributions that he would make personally and on which he would enjoy full income tax relief.

The top half of Table 6 shows exactly the same thing for a range of different starting salaries. In each case we assume the salary grows by 3% per year, the employer makes a 5% pension contribution for five years and the money grows by 7% per year tax free.

For example, if your salary is £30,000 now and you lose out on five years' worth of employer contributions and an additional 15 years of tax-free growth on that money, the total loss to your pension pot after 20 years will be £26,932.

The second half of the table shows exactly the same thing except this time we assume the employee is not a member of the workplace pension scheme for 10 years. For example, if your salary is £30,000 now and you lose out on 10 years' worth of employer contributions and an additional 10 years of tax-free growth on that money, the total loss to your pension pot after 20 years will be £49,193.

112

Table 6
5% Employer Pension Contribution
Long-term Value

Employer Contributions for 5 Years
Value after...

Starting Salary £	10 Years £	20 Years £	30 Years £	40 Years £
20,000	9127	17,955	35,320	69,480
30,000	13,691	26,932	52,980	104,220
40,000	18,255	35,910	70,640	138,959
50,000	22,818	44,887	88,300	173,699
60,000	27,382	53,865	105,960	208,439
70,000	31,946	62,842	123,620	243,179
80,000	36,509	71,820	141,280	277,919
90,000	41,073	80,797	158,940	312,659
100,000	45,637	89,774	176,600	347,399

Employer Contributions for 10 Years
Value after...

Starting Salary £	10 Years £	20 Years £	30 Years £	40 Years £
20,000	16,672	32,795	64,514	126,908
30,000	25,007	49,193	96,770	190,362
40,000	33,343	65,591	129,027	253,816
50,000	41,679	81,989	161,284	317,270
60,000	50,015	98,386	193,541	380,724
70,000	58,350	114,784	225,798	444,178
80,000	66,686	131,182	258,054	507,632
90,000	75,022	147,579	290,311	571,086
100,000	83,358	163,977	322,568	634,540

Different Employer Pension Contributions

Different employers pay different amounts into their employees' pensions.

To find out how much a bigger or smaller employer contribution is worth all you have to do is scale the numbers in Table 6 up or down.

For example, if the employer offers a 10% contribution you simply double the numbers. In this case Douglas, with a starting salary of £50,000 and no contributions for five years, will have lost £89,774 after 20 years (£44,887 x 2).

If the employer offers an 8% contribution you multiply the numbers by 1.6 (found by dividing 8 by 5).

If the employer offers a 3% contribution you multiply the numbers by 0.6 (found by dividing 3 by 5).

... and so on.

Putting Things in Perspective

The numbers in the table are quite large and imply that, by not belonging to a workplace pension scheme, and not receiving pension contributions from your employer, you may be losing a lot of free money.

However, it's important to put the figures in perspective. Let's say Douglas is 35 years old and 30 years away from retirement. By not receiving employer pension contributions for five years, his pension pot will have lost £88,300 of free money after 30 years.

However, by that time his salary will have grown to £117,828 (growing at just 3% per year to compensate for inflation). What this means is that not contributing to his employer's pension for five years has cost him around nine months' salary.

Is this a price worth paying? Only Douglas can answer that.

And what if Douglas is a high flier and his pay increases by more than inflation, as he climbs the corporate ladder?

If we assume his salary grows by 7% per year (i.e. at the same pace as his investments) we find that after 30 years he is sitting on a salary of £355,713. And his pension pot will have lost out on £95,153 worth of employer contributions.

In total Douglas will have lost just over three months' pay by not receiving pension contributions from his employer for five years.

Personally, I am of the opinion that anyone offered free cash by their employer should grasp the opportunity with open arms.

BUT...

If you do not belong to your workplace pension scheme for just a few years, this may not have a significant effect on your income in retirement IF you expect your salary to grow rapidly, resulting in bigger employer pension contributions in later years.

Part 6

Salary Sacrifice Pensions

Chapter 20

Introduction to Salary Sacrifice Pensions

How would you like to increase your pension pot by up to 34%, with the taxman footing the entire bill? It seems too good to be true but this result can be achieved if you stop making pension contributions *personally* and get your employer to make them for you.

This set-up is known as salary sacrifice (also salary exchange or 'smart pensions') and is used by some of the country's biggest companies, universities and other organisations, including BT, Tesco and the BBC.

In my opinion, a salary sacrifice pension is the best tax-saving opportunity available to regular salaried employees. That's why I've decided to include a dedicated section on them in this guide.

So how does it work? Salary sacrifice is all about saving *national insurance*, on top of the income tax relief you already receive when you make pension contributions.

Most people only enjoy income tax relief when they contribute to a pension. The income tax relief is attractive but it's not the maximum amount of tax relief available. When an employee contributes personally to a pension plan there is no refund of all the national insurance paid by both the employee and the employer. As much as £258 of national insurance is paid by the employee and employer on £1,000 of salary.

With salary sacrifice arrangements, it is possible to put a stop to these national insurance payments because your employer makes your pension contributions for you.

Pension contributions paid by employers are exempt from national insurance.

The national insurance savings can then be added to your pension pot.

Sacrificing Salary, Not Income

Because the employer has to pay the employee's pension contributions, the employee in return has to sacrifice some salary.

However, it's important to stress that the employee's net take-home pay does not fall – it remains exactly the same.

With salary sacrifice there are no losers: Both the employee and employer can save money. The only loser is the taxman!

Company Pension Scheme Not Required

It is not necessary to belong to some sort of company pension scheme. Salary sacrifice works with almost all pension plans including:

- Self-invested personal pensions (SIPPs)
- Personal pensions (group and individual plans)
- Stakeholder pensions (group and individual plans)
- Occupational pension schemes

The main consideration is that the plan must be able to accept employer contributions. Many SIPP providers have special forms for this purpose.

Salary sacrifice can be used by most employees. However, sole traders and other self-employed individuals cannot use salary sacrifice because there is no employer to make pension contributions on their behalf.

There has to be an employer/employee relationship for a salary sacrifice arrangement to be successful.

Chapter 21

Income Tax & National Insurance: A Five-Minute Primer

There are lots of examples in the chapters that follow and many of them use income tax and national insurance rates and allowances.

In this chapter I'm going to briefly explain how income tax and national insurance are calculated for the average salary-earning employee.

This should make the examples easier to understand (and slightly less painful!).

Calculating Income Tax

For the 2014/15 tax year, starting on 6 April 2014, most employees pay income tax as follows:

- 0% on the first £10,000   Personal allowance
- 20% on the next £31,865   Basic-rate band
- 40% above £41,865   Higher-rate threshold

Generally speaking, if you earn more than £41,865 you are a higher-rate taxpayer; if you earn less you are a basic-rate taxpayer.

Example – Basic-Rate Taxpayer

John earns a salary of £30,000. His income tax for 2014/15 can be calculated as follows:

- *0% on the first £10,000 = £0*
- *20% on the next £20,000 = £4,000*

Total income tax bill: £4,000

Example – Higher-Rate Taxpayer

Jane earns a salary of £60,000. Her income tax for 2014/15 can be calculated as follows:

- *0% on the first £10,000 = £0*
- *20% on the next £31,865 = £6,373*
- *40% on the final £18,135 = £7,254*

Total income tax bill: £13,627

Income above £100,000 and £150,000

When your income exceeds £100,000 your tax-free personal allowance is gradually withdrawn and when your income exceeds £150,000 you also start paying tax at 45%.

Calculating National Insurance

For the 2014/15 tax year employees pay national insurance as follows:

- 0%   on the first   £7,956   Earnings threshold
- 12%   on the next   £33,909
- 2%   above   £41,865   Upper earnings limit

Employers pay 13.8% national insurance on every single pound the employee earns over £7,956. There is no cap.

You probably don't lose much sleep over your employer's national insurance bill. However, employer's national insurance is a tax on YOUR income. If it didn't exist your employer would be able to pay you a higher salary.

Here are John and Jane's national insurance calculations:

Example – Basic-Rate Taxpayer

John earns a salary of £30,000. His national insurance for 2014/15 can be calculated as follows:

- *0% on the first £7,956 = £0*
- *12% on the next £22,044 = £2,645*

John's national insurance bill: £2,645

John's employer pays national insurance on John's salary as follows:

- *0% on the first £7,956 = £0*
- *13.8% on the next £22,044 = £3,042*

John's employer's national insurance bill: £3,042

Example – Higher-Rate Taxpayer

Jane earns a salary of £60,000. Her national insurance for 2014/15 can be calculated as follows:

- *0% on the first £7,956 = £0*
- *12% on the next £33,909 = £4,069*
- *2% on the final £18,135 = £363*

Jane's national insurance bill: £4,432

Her employer's national insurance is:

- *0% on the first £7,956 = £0*
- *13.8% on the next £52,044 = £7,182*

Jane's employer's national insurance bill: £7,182

Tax Bills Combined

John and Jane's tax bills can be summarised as follows:

John – Basic-rate Taxpayer – £30,000

	£
Income tax	4,000
Employee's national insurance	2,645
Employer's national insurance	3,042
Total taxes	**9,687**

Jane – Higher-rate Taxpayer – £60,000

	£
Income tax	13,627
Employee's national insurance	4,432
Employer's national insurance	7,182
Total taxes	**25,241**

When you include employer's national insurance it's startling how much tax is paid even by those on relatively modest incomes. Direct taxes on John's income come to 32%.

Jane's £60,000 salary is not low by any standards but you wouldn't describe her as a high income earner either. Nevertheless an amount equivalent to 42% of her salary is paid in direct taxes on her income.

Chapter 22

Salary Sacrifice Case Study: Basic-Rate Taxpayer

Introduction

We are going to follow the same John from the previous chapter and show how his total pension pot can be increased by 34% with a salary sacrifice pension.

Remember John earns £30,000 and is a basic-rate taxpayer. Basic-rate taxpayers pay 20% income tax and 12% national insurance.

John's Retirement Savings

John pays income tax of £4,000 and national insurance of £2,645 on his £30,000 salary.

Let's say he also puts £1,000 into a savings account (just over 3% of his salary).

After deducting his taxes and savings he is left with a disposable income of £22,355.

John faces a dilemma. He knows he's not saving much but he also has children to support and feels he cannot live on a penny less than £22,355.

On the advice of a friend, John starts saving into a pension plan. He contributes £1,000 and the taxman tops this up with an extra £250 of free cash (basic-rate tax relief), bringing John's total pension saving to £1,250.

In summary, John's pension saving is £1,250 per year, even though his personal contribution is only £1,000. The amount he saves has increased by 25%.

Avoiding National Insurance

This is not a bad outcome but John can do much better.

So far he has enjoyed full *income tax* relief on his pension contributions. However, income tax is not the only tax John pays. He also pays 12% national insurance on most of his salary and his employer pays 13.8%.

Unfortunately, there is no national insurance relief for pension contributions made personally by employees like John. However, there is full national insurance relief for pension contributions made by employers.

John therefore decides to stop contributing personally to his pension and asks his employer to make the contributions for him. In return, John agrees to sacrifice some salary.

John's Salary Sacrifice

John sacrifices £1,470, which takes his salary from £30,000 to £28,530 (we will explain why he sacrifices this amount in Chapter 24).

After deducting income tax and national insurance on £28,530 he is still left with £22,355 – the exact amount of income we know he needs to live on.

John's employer pays the £1,470 of sacrificed salary directly into John's pension plan. His employer also contributes an additional £203, representing the employer's national insurance saving:

£1,470 x 13.8% = £203

Remember, employers pay national insurance on salaries but not on pension contributions.

The amount going into John's pension pot now is £1,673.

In summary, John still has £22,355 of take-home pay, just as before, but his pension contribution has increased from £1,250 to £1,673 – an increase of 34%.

Remember, before John started contributing to a pension plan he was not enjoying any national insurance relief OR income tax relief and was saving just £1,000 per year.

Now he is enjoying full income tax and national insurance relief and the amount he saves has increased by 67%.

In summary, John is avoiding 20% income tax, 12% employee's national insurance and 13.8% employer's national insurance on the money paid into his pension plan.

A summary of the number crunching can be found on the next page.

John's Take Home Pay Stays the Same

	Before Salary Sacrifice	After Salary Sacrifice
	£	£
Salary	30,000	28,530
Less:		
Income tax	4,000	3,706
National insurance	2,645	2,469
Pension contribution	1,000	0
Disposable income	**22,355**	**22,355**

... But His Pension Pot Increases By 34%

	Before Salary Sacrifice	After Salary Sacrifice
	£	£
Employee contribution	1,000	-
Taxman's top up	250	-
Employer contribution	-	1,470
Employer's NI saving	-	203
Total	**1,250**	**1,673**

Long-Term Picture

So far we have taken a one-year snapshot. Pension plans are long-term savings vehicles, so it's important to examine how salary sacrifice affects John's pension pot over a period of, say, 10 years.

The table below shows how John's pension pot grows with and without salary sacrifice.

Year	Without Sacrifice £	With Sacrifice £
1	1,250	1,673
2	2,588	3,463
3	4,019	5,379
4	5,550	7,428
5	7,188	9,621
6	8,942	11,967
7	10,818	14,478
8	12,825	17,165
9	14,972	20,039
10	17,271	23,115

There are a couple of assumptions behind these numbers:

- **John's annual pension contribution is the same every year**. This assumption keeps things simple but does not affect what the example seeks to illustrate. So John's pension contribution every year is £1,250 (without salary sacrifice) and £1,673 (with salary sacrifice).

- **John's investments grow by 7% per year tax free**. This assumption also does not affect what the example is trying to illustrate.

To explain how each number in the table is calculated let's look at John's position without salary sacrifice and step forward to year two. The number in the table is £2,588. This is made up of his contribution in year one, plus 7% growth on that contribution, plus his contribution in year two:

$$£1,250 + £88 + £1,250 = £2,588$$

In year 10 John will have £17,271 in his pension pot without salary sacrifice, compared with £23,115 with salary sacrifice. Clearly, salary sacrifice will leave him significantly better off.

The pound amounts, however, are largely meaningless to anyone except John. Your own pension contributions will be either bigger or smaller than his, your investments will probably grow at a different rate and you may be interested in a period lasting longer or shorter than 10 years.

However, what IS relevant is the *percentage difference* between the two columns in the table. Every year it is exactly the same: 34%!

This implies the following for basic-rate taxpayers who use salary sacrifice:

No matter how much you save, and for how long, and no matter how well your investments perform, you will end up with a 34% bigger pension pot.

In other words, a basic-rate taxpayer who uses salary sacrifice will have 34% more retirement money than someone who does not.

So if your pension pot would have been, say, £100,000 without salary sacrifice, it will be £134,000 with salary sacrifice. If your pension pot would have been £200,000 without salary sacrifice, it will be £268,000 with salary sacrifice. If your pension pot would have been £300,000 without salary sacrifice it will be £402,000 with salary sacrifice... and so on.

When you stop and think about it, the implications are enormous. Salary sacrifice could have a HUGE impact on your quality of life when you retire.

Chapter 23

Salary Sacrifice Case Study: Higher-Rate Taxpayer

Introduction

In this chapter we are going to follow the same Jane from Chapter 21 and show you how she can boost her pension pot with a salary sacrifice arrangement.

Remember, Jane earns £60,000 and is a higher-rate taxpayer. Higher-rate taxpayers pay 40% income tax and 2% national insurance on their earnings over £41,865.

Jane's Retirement Savings

We know from Chapter 21 that Jane's income tax and national insurance bill comes to £18,059. She puts £1,800 (3% of her salary) into a savings account, which leaves her with a disposable income of £40,141.

Jane has various financial commitments and feels that she cannot live on a penny less than £40,141.

She decides to put her savings into a pension plan instead. She contributes £2,400 and the taxman tops this up with an extra £600 of free cash (her basic-rate tax relief), bringing Jane's total pension saving to £3,000.

Jane can afford to increase the amount she saves from £1,800 to £2,400 because she also receives a £600 income tax refund when she submits her tax return (her higher-rate tax relief).

In summary, Jane saves £3,000 in her pension, even though her personal contribution is only £1,800.

The amount she saves has increased by 67%.

Avoiding National Insurance

So far, Jane has enjoyed full *income tax* relief on her pension contributions but no national insurance relief because, as we know, there is no national insurance relief for pension contributions made by employees.

So Jane decides to stop contributing personally and asks her employer to make the contributions directly.

In return, Jane agrees to sacrifice £3,103 of salary which takes her from £60,000 to £56,897 – I will explain why she sacrifices this exact amount in Chapter 24.

After deducting income tax and national insurance she is left with £40,141 – the exact amount we know she needs to live on.

Jane's employer pays the £3,103 of sacrificed salary directly into her pension plan. Her employer also contributes the employer's national insurance saving, which comes to £428 (£3,103 x 13.8%).

Jane's total pension contribution is now £3,531 and has increased by 18%.

It's not as much as the 34% increase enjoyed by John, the basic-rate taxpayer, because higher-rate taxpayers generally only save 2% national insurance on the salary they sacrifice, whereas basic-rate taxpayers save 12%.

Both types of taxpayer, however, can benefit from their employers' 13.8% national insurance saving.

Although Jane's pension contribution hasn't increased as much as John's in *percentage* terms, it has increased more in pounds and pence.

Her pension contribution has risen by £531, compared with John's rise of £423.

Remember Jane hasn't paid a single penny out of her own pocket to achieve this result!

Total Tax Savings

It is also important to remember that Jane is enjoying much more *income tax* relief than John (40% as opposed to 20%). Remember, before Jane started contributing to a pension plan she was not enjoying any national insurance relief OR income tax relief and was saving just £1,800 per year. Now she is enjoying full income tax and national insurance relief and the amount she saves is £3,531 – an increase of 96%.

In summary, Jane is avoiding 40% income tax, 2% employee's national insurance and 13.8% employer's national insurance on the money she contributes to her pension plan. She is still left with the same amount of take-home pay but her retirement saving has increased as follows:

£1,800

No pension

↓

£3,000

Pension with income tax relief
No national insurance relief

↓

£3,531

Pension with income tax relief
__and__ national insurance relief

It's also worth stating that Jane, with a salary of £60,000, will effectively lose all of her child benefit every year if she isn't making any pension contributions and is the household's highest earner (see Chapter 16). By sacrificing roughly £3,100 of salary, she gets to claw back 31% of her child benefit. That's an additional saving of £549 per year if she has two children, on top of all the income tax and national insurance saved.

Jane's Take Home Pay Stays the Same

	Before Salary Sacrifice	After Salary Sacrifice
	£	£
Salary	60,000	56,897
Less:		
Income tax	13,027*	12,386
National insurance	4,432	4,370
Pension contribution	2,400	0
Disposable income	**40,141**	**40,141**

... But Her Pension Pot Increases By 18%

	Before Salary Sacrifice	After Salary Sacrifice
	£	£
Employee contribution	2,400	-
Taxman's top up	600	-
Employer contribution	-	3,103
Employer's NI saving	-	428
Total	**3,000**	**3,531**

* Reduced by £600 higher-rate income tax relief.

Long-Term Benefits – Higher-Rate Taxpayers

Again, the above example is a one-year snapshot. Pension plans are long-term savings vehicles, so let's examine how salary sacrifice affects Jane's pension pot over a period of 10 years.

The table below shows how Jane's pension pot grows with and without salary sacrifice.

Year	Before Sacrifice £	After Sacrifice £
1	3,000	3,531
2	6,210	7,309
3	9,645	11,352
4	13,320	15,677
5	17,252	20,306
6	21,460	25,258
7	25,962	30,557
8	30,779	36,227
9	35,934	42,294
10	41,449	48,786

The assumptions are the same as for John in the previous case study: Jane's annual pension contribution stays the same each year (£3,000 without salary sacrifice and £3,531 with salary sacrifice) and her investments grow by 7% per year tax free.

In year 10 Jane will have £41,449 in her pension pot without salary sacrifice compared with £48,786 with salary sacrifice.

Again, as with John, what is relevant is the *percentage* difference between the two columns in the table. Every year it is exactly the same: 18%.

This implies the following for higher-rate taxpayers who use salary sacrifice:

No matter how much you save, and for how long, and no matter how well your investments perform, you will end up with an 18% bigger pension pot.

Chapter 24

Calculating How Much YOU Can Save

So much for John and Jane. In this chapter I am going to show you how to do the number crunching for your personal situation and show you how much better off you could be, in pounds and pence, with a salary sacrifice pension.

There are three steps here:

1. Calculate how much salary you need to sacrifice. This amount will be paid into your pension by your employer. The aim here is to make sure your after-tax disposable income does not decrease.

2. Multiply (1) by 13.8%. This is your employer's national insurance saving and is also added to your pension pot.

3. Compare (1) + (2) with your current gross pension contribution.

The calculation is different for basic-rate taxpayers and higher-rate taxpayers (those earning more than £41,865 in the current tax year) because these two groups pay different amounts of income tax and national insurance.

Basic-Rate Taxpayers

Let's say you are a basic-rate taxpayer and personally contribute £100 to your pension plan. To get that £100 in your hands you will have had to earn salary of £147:

£147 _less_ 20% income tax _less_ 12% national insurance = £100

So if you give up £147 of salary *and* stop making pension contributions you will still have exactly the same amount of disposable income.

So, to calculate how much salary you should sacrifice, simply take your current cash pension contribution (the amount you personally contribute, before the taxman tops it up) and add back the 20% income tax and 12% national insurance you have paid.

To do this quickly, simply divide your cash pension contribution by 0.68:

$$\frac{\text{Cash Pension Contribution}}{0.68}$$

Example
John is a basic-rate taxpayer and personally contributes £1,000 to his pension plan annually. His total gross contribution, including the taxman's top up, is £1,250. The amount of salary John needs to sacrifice is calculated as follows:

$$\frac{£1,000}{0.68}$$

$$= £1,470$$

If John stops contributing to his pension plan and sacrifices this amount of salary, his disposable income will remain exactly the same.

His employer will contribute £1,470 to his pension plan plus an extra £203 (£1,470 x 13.8%), representing the employer's national insurance saving. His total pension contribution will be £1,673.

Table 7 shows the same calculation for a whole range of different pension contributions. For example, if you are contributing £3,000 per year you will be £1,271 better off, if you are contributing £6,000 per year you will be £2,541 better off... and so on.

As a general rule, your pension savings will be 34% higher than before if you are a basic-rate taxpayer.

TABLE 7
Sample Pension Increases: Basic-Rate Taxpayers

Cash Contribution (1) £	Gross Contribution (2) £	Salary Sacrifice (3) £	New Contribution (4) £	Increase (5) £
500	625	735	837	212
750	938	1,103	1,255	318
1,000	1,250	1,470	1,673	423
1,250	1,563	1,838	2,092	529
1,500	1,875	2,206	2,510	635
1,750	2,188	2,574	2,929	741
2,000	2,500	2,941	3,347	847
2,250	2,813	3,309	3,765	953
2,500	3,125	3,676	4,184	1,059
2,750	3,438	4,044	4,602	1,165
3,000	3,750	4,412	5,021	1,271
3,500	4,375	5,147	5,857	1,482
4,000	5,000	5,882	6,694	1,694
4,500	5,625	6,618	7,531	1,906
5,000	6,250	7,353	8,368	2,118
5,500	6,875	8,088	9,204	2,329
6,000	7,500	8,824	10,041	2,541
6,500	8,125	9,559	10,878	2,753
7,000	8,750	10,294	11,715	2,965
7,500	9,375	11,029	12,551	3,176
8,000	10,000	11,765	13,388	3,388
8,500	10,625	12,500	14,225	3,600
9,000	11,250	13,235	15,062	3,812
9,500	11,875	13,971	15,899	4,024
10,000	12,500	14,706	16,735	4,235

Column descriptions:

1) Cash Contribution. A range of cash pension contributions, _before_ the taxman's top up payment is added.

2) Gross Contribution. Found by dividing (1) by 0.8. This is the total gross pension contribution, ie with the taxman's top up payment added.

3) Salary Sacrifice. Found by dividing (1) by 0.68. The amount of salary you have to sacrifice while keeping your take-home pay constant.

4) New Contribution. This is your new salary sacrifice pension contribution which is simply column (3) plus 13.8%, representing the employer's national insurance saving.

5) Increase. The increase in pension saving: (4) minus (2). Always 34%.

Your Long-Term Savings – Basic Rate Taxpayer

So much for the *annual* savings. How much better off are you likely to be after a longer period – say 10 years – with a salary sacrifice pension?

Table 8 attempts to answer this question for a whole range of annual pension contributions and illustrates the potential savings in pounds and pence.

It's the fourth column in Table 8 that is the important one – it shows you in pounds and pence how much better off you could be with a salary sacrifice pension after 10 years.

A number of assumptions have been used to crunch the numbers. First, to keep things simple, it is assumed that the amount saved remains the same from year to year.

Second, it is assumed that the pension investments grow by 7% per year. Neither assumption makes a huge amount of difference to the outcome.

TABLE 8
Savings after 10 Years: Basic-Rate Taxpayers

Annual Cash Contribution £	Pension Pot No Sacrifice £	Pension Pot With Sacrifice £	Pension Pot Increase £
500	8,635	11,561	2,926
750	12,953	17,342	4,389
1,000	17,271	23,129	5,858
1,250	21,588	28,903	7,315
1,500	25,906	34,683	8,778
1,750	30,223	40,464	10,240
2,000	34,541	46,244	11,703
2,250	38,859	52,025	13,166
2,500	43,176	57,806	14,629
2,750	47,494	63,586	16,092
3,000	51,812	69,367	17,555
3,500	60,447	80,928	20,481
4,000	69,082	92,489	23,407
4,500	77,718	104,050	26,333
5,000	86,353	115,611	29,258
5,500	94,988	127,172	32,184
6,000	103,623	138,733	35,110
6,500	112,259	150,295	38,036
7,000	120,894	161,856	40,962
7,500	129,529	173,417	43,888
8,000	138,164	184,978	46,813
8,500	146,800	196,539	49,739
9,000	155,435	208,100	52,665
9,500	164,070	219,661	55,591
10,000	172,706	231,222	58,517

Assumptions:

- Pension investments grow by 7% per year
- No increase in annual pension contribution

Let's take a look at a sample number from the table. If you personally contribute £4,000 per year to your pension plan, you will end up with £69,082 after 10 years. But if you have a salary sacrifice pension you will end up with £92,489 – an increase of £23,407.

That's quite a big increase. Remember this money is completely **free**! You would not have to save a single penny extra to enjoy this boost to your retirement savings.

The extra money comes about because you and your employer are saving national insurance.

Ultra Long-Term Savings – Basic-Rate Taxpayers

I used a 10-year period in Table 8 because I believe most people do not look much further into the future than this.

In reality, pension plans are often *ultra long-term* savings vehicles and it is possible you will be saving for much longer than 10 years – maybe 20 years, 30 years, 40 years… or even longer!

With this in mind it's important to note that a basic-rate taxpayer (or a couple who are both basic-rate taxpayers) saving £5,000 per year and switching to a salary sacrifice pension will end up with:

- An **extra** £87,000 after 20 years

- An **extra** £200,000 after 30 years

- An **extra** £423,000 after 40 years

By simply changing the way your pension contributions are paid you could end up with an **extra** £87,000 or even £423,000, without paying a single penny extra into your pension plan.

A pension contribution of £5,000 per year is hardly onerous. For a couple it represents a monthly contribution of around £200 each.

Higher-Rate Taxpayers

In this section I'm going to show you how to do the number crunching for your personal situation if you are a higher-rate taxpayer and show you how much better off you could be, in pounds and pence, with a salary sacrifice pension.

First of all we have to calculate how much salary you should sacrifice so that you end up with exactly the same amount of after-tax disposable income.

Let's say you are a higher-rate taxpayer and personally contribute £100 to your pension. The gross contribution is £125 (£100/0.8) and you will receive £25 of higher-rate relief (£125 x 20%). So the actual cost to you is just £75 (£100 - £25).

To get £75 of income in your hands you will have had to earn £129 of salary:

£129 _less_ 40% income tax _less_ 2% national insurance = £75

So if you sacrifice £129 of salary and stop making pension contributions you will still have exactly the same amount of disposable income to spend.

To perform the same calculation for yourself and calculate exactly how much salary you need to sacrifice just follow these two simple steps:

- **Step 1.** Multiply the amount you personally contribute to your pension by 0.75 – the resulting number is what your pension contributions are actually costing you and takes into account your higher-rate relief.

- **Step 2.** Add back the 40% income tax and 2% national insurance you have paid on this income. To do this divide the result from Step 1 by 0.58:

$$\frac{\text{Step 1}}{0.58}$$

Example

Jane, a higher-rate taxpayer, personally contributes £2,400 per year to her pension. The taxman tops this up with £600, so her gross pension contribution is £3,000. Jane's salary sacrifice is calculated as follows:

- **Step 1.** *Multiply the amount she personally contributes to her pension by 0.75:*

$$£2,400 \times 0.75 = £1,800$$

- **Step 2.** *Add back her 40% income tax and 2% national insurance by dividing the result by 0.58:*

$$£1,800/0.58 = £3,103$$

This is the amount of income Jane has to sacrifice. If she sacrifices £3,103 of salary and stops contributing to her pension plan, her disposable income will remain exactly the same.

Her employer will contribute £3,103 to her pension plan, plus an extra £428 (£3,103 x 13.8%). This is the employer's national insurance saving. Her total pension contribution is now £3,531.

Table 9 shows the same calculation for a whole range of different pension contributions. The columns can be described as follows:

1) Cash Contribution. Cash pension contribution _before_ the taxman's top up payment is added.

2) Total Contribution. Found by dividing (1) by 0.8. This is the gross pension contribution, ie with taxman's top up added.

3) Salary Sacrifice. Found by dividing the pension contribution net of all tax relief by 0.58 – the amount of salary a higher-rate taxpayer has to sacrifice while keeping take-home pay constant.

4) New Contribution. This is your new salary sacrifice pension contribution amount, which is simply column (3) plus an extra 13.8%, representing the employer's national insurance saving.

5) Increase. The increase in pension saving: (4) minus (2). In each case the new pension contribution (4) is 18% higher than the old one (2).

TABLE 9
Sample Pension Increases: Higher-Rate Taxpayers

Cash Contribution (1) £	Total Contribution (2) £	Salary Sacrifice (3) £	New Contribution (4) £	Increase (5) £
500	625	647	736	111
750	938	970	1,104	166
1,000	1,250	1,293	1,472	222
1,250	1,563	1,616	1,839	277
1,500	1,875	1,940	2,207	332
1,750	2,188	2,263	2,575	388
2,000	2,500	2,586	2,943	443
2,250	2,813	2,909	3,311	498
2,500	3,125	3,233	3,679	554
2,750	3,438	3,556	4,047	609
3,000	3,750	3,879	4,415	665
3,500	4,375	4,526	5,150	775
4,000	5,000	5,172	5,886	886
4,500	5,625	5,819	6,622	997
5,000	6,250	6,466	7,358	1,108
5,500	6,875	7,112	8,094	1,219
6,000	7,500	7,759	8,829	1,329
6,500	8,125	8,405	9,565	1,440
7,000	8,750	9,052	10,301	1,551
7,500	9,375	9,698	11,037	1,662
8,000	10,000	10,345	11,772	1,772
8,500	10,625	10,991	12,508	1,883
9,000	11,250	11,638	13,244	1,994
9,500	11,875	12,284	13,980	2,105
10,000	12,500	12,931	14,716	2,216
10,500	13,125	13,578	15,451	2,326
11,000	13,750	14,224	16,187	2,437
11,500	14,375	14,871	16,923	2,548
12,000	15,000	15,517	17,659	2,659
12,500	15,625	16,164	18,394	2,769
13,000	16,250	16,810	19,130	2,880
13,500	16,875	17,457	19,866	2,991
14,000	17,500	18,103	20,602	3,102
14,500	18,125	18,750	21,338	3,213
15,000	18,750	19,397	22,073	3,323
16,000	20,000	20,690	23,545	3,545
17,000	21,250	21,983	25,016	3,766
18,000	22,500	23,276	26,488	3,988
19,000	23,750	24,569	27,959	4,209
20,000	25,000	25,862	29,431	4,431

The table is easy to use. For example, if you are currently personally contributing £6,000 per year to your pension plan, you will be £1,329 better off with a salary sacrifice pension.

There are two important points to remember about this table:

- First, you will enjoy this free increase to you pension pot **every year.**

- Second, this is just your national insurance saving. As a higher-rate taxpayer you will also be enjoying 40% income tax relief on your pension contributions.

  For example, a higher-rate taxpayer who personally contributes £6,000 to a pension plan will receive a £1,500 income tax refund from the taxman so the actual cost is just £4,500. The taxman's top-up will take the total pension contribution to £7,500. With salary sacrifice the pension contribution then goes up to £8,829 without costing you a penny extra.

  So what you have is a pension contribution of £8,829 that has effectively cost just £4,500.

Long-Term Savings – Higher Rate Taxpayers

So much for your *annual* savings. How much better off are you likely to be after a longer period – say 10 years – with a salary sacrifice pension?

Table 10 attempts to answer this question for a whole range of annual pension contributions and illustrates the potential savings in pounds and pence for a higher-rate taxpayer.

It's the fourth column in Table 10 that is the important one – it shows you in pounds and pence how much better off you could be with a salary sacrifice pension after 10 years.

Again a number of assumptions have been used to crunch the numbers. First, to keep things simple, it is assumed that the amount saved remains the same from year to year. Second, it is assumed that the pension investments grow by 7% per year.

Neither assumption makes a huge amount of difference to the outcome.

Let's take a look at a sample number from the table. If you personally contribute £6,000 per year to your pension plan, you will end up with £103,623 after 10 years. But if you have a salary sacrifice pension you will end up with £121,990 – an increase of £18,367.

That's quite a big increase. Remember this money is completely **free**! You would not have to save a single penny extra to enjoy this boost to your retirement savings.

The extra money comes about because you and your employer are saving national insurance.

TABLE 10
Savings after 10 Years: Higher-Rate Taxpayers

Annual Cash Contribution £	Pension Pot No Sacrifice £	Pension Pot With Sacrifice £	Pension Pot Increase £
500	8,635	10,166	1,531
750	12,953	15,249	2,296
1,000	17,271	20,332	3,061
1,250	21,588	25,415	3,826
1,500	25,906	30,497	4,592
1,750	30,223	35,580	5,357
2,000	34,541	40,663	6,122
2,250	38,859	45,746	6,887
2,500	43,176	50,829	7,653
2,750	47,494	55,912	8,418
3,000	51,812	60,995	9,183
3,500	60,447	71,161	10,714
4,000	69,082	81,326	12,244
4,500	77,718	91,492	13,775
5,000	86,353	101,658	15,305
5,500	94,988	111,824	16,836
6,000	103,623	121,990	18,367
6,500	112,259	132,156	19,897
7,000	120,894	142,321	21,427
7,500	129,529	152,487	22,958
8,000	138,164	162,653	24,488
8,500	146,800	172,819	26,019
9,000	155,435	182,985	27,550
9,500	164,070	193,150	29,080
10,000	172,706	203,316	30,611
10,500	181,341	213,482	32,141
11,000	189,976	223,648	33,672
11,500	198,611	233,814	35,202
12,000	207,247	243,979	36,733
12,500	215,882	254,145	38,263
13,000	224,517	264,311	39,794
13,500	233,153	274,477	41,324
14,000	241,788	284,643	42,855
14,500	250,423	294,808	44,385
15,000	259,058	304,974	45,916
16,000	276,329	325,306	48,977
17,000	293,600	345,638	52,038
18,000	310,870	365,969	55,099
19,000	328,141	386,301	58,160
20,000	345,411	406,632	61,221

Ultra Long-Term Savings – Higher-Rate Taxpayers

I used a 10-year period to construct Table 10.

Of course pension plans are ultra long-term savings vehicles and it is possible you will be saving for longer than 10 years – maybe 20 years, 30 years, or 40 years.

With this in mind it's interesting to note that a higher-rate taxpayer saving £7,500 per year who switches to a salary sacrifice pension will end up with:

- An **extra** £68,000 after 20 years

- An **extra** £157,000 after 30 years

- An **extra** £332,000 after 40 years

Again, I find these results staggering. By simply changing the way your pension contributions are paid you could end up with an **extra** £68,000 or even £332,000, without paying a single penny extra into your pension plan.

A pension contribution of £7,500 per year is hardly onerous. For a couple who are both higher-rate taxpayers it represents a monthly contribution of just over £300 each.

Chapter 25

How to Convince Your Employer

After 23 years in the tax publishing business one thing I have learnt is that most tax breaks come with a catch.

With salary sacrifice pensions the catch is you need your employer's co-operation. A salary sacrifice pension arrangement will only work if your employer agrees to do the necessary paperwork (see Chapter 27), reduce your salary and contribute to your pension plan.

How much bargaining power you have with your employer will, of course, depend on how big the company is and how senior you are.

If you are a senior executive at a small or medium-sized company, you should find it relatively easy to get your employer to introduce a salary sacrifice arrangement. If you are a junior employee at a multinational corporation your chances are probably slim.

However, because a salary sacrifice arrangement could increase your pension pot by tens of thousands of pounds and have a huge impact on your quality of life when you retire, I believe it's worth fighting for tooth and nail.

Remember, to implement a salary sacrifice arrangement it is NOT necessary for your employer to set up some sort of company pension scheme. Salary sacrifice also works with personal pensions and SIPPs etc.

Fortunately, there are several arguments you can use to convince your employer:

Argument #1 Other Employers Are Doing It

Salary sacrifice pensions are available from some of the country's biggest and most reputable companies, universities and other organisations, including BT, Tesco and the BBC.

To stay competitive in the jobs market your employer should also be offering this benefit.

Argument #2 Easy to Implement

As we will see in Chapter 27, the paperwork is all relatively straightforward and may only have to be done once.

Argument #3 Auto Enrolment

The Government is already rolling out compulsory employer pension contributions (see Chapter 18).

If your employer starts making pension contributions on your behalf now (funded by you via a salary sacrifice) he may not have to make any extra payments when compulsory contributions are eventually introduced.

Argument #4 Giving Employees a FREE Pay Increase

This is by far the most powerful argument you can use to convince your employer to introduce a salary sacrifice pension arrangement.

The employee effectively receives a pay increase that doesn't cost the employer anything. The taxman foots the entire bill.

What rational employer would turn down such an opportunity?

Sharing the Savings with Your Employer

If you are struggling to convince your employer to introduce a salary sacrifice pension arrangement, you can offer to share the national insurance savings.

Remember there are two types of national insurance: the type the employee pays and the type the employer pays.

In all the examples so far we have assumed that both the employee's and employer's national insurance savings are paid into the employee's pension plan.

However, to convince your employer to introduce a salary sacrifice pension arrangement you may have to appeal to his selfish side and offer to share the national insurance savings.

Your employer pays 13.8% national insurance on every penny you earn over £7,956 (2014/15 figures). It may be necessary to offer your employer, say, half of the employer's national insurance saving (6.9% of the salary sacrifice amount) to co-operate with you.

Ideally you should negotiate to have your employer share the national insurance savings for just one year, perhaps to compensate him for time spent doing the necessary paperwork. However, even if your employer insists on a permanent national insurance share, you will still be far better off in most cases with a salary sacrifice pension arrangement.

Table 11 illustrates the annual benefit of a salary sacrifice arrangement for a whole range of different pension contribution amounts for basic-rate taxpayers. The table is exactly the same as Table 7 in Chapter 24, except for columns 4 and 5. In column 4 only half the employer's national insurance saving is added to the employee's pension plan (6.9% instead of 13.8%).

Column 5 is the important one and shows how much better off a basic-rate taxpayer will be every year with a salary sacrifice arrangement if only half the employer's national insurance saving is paid into the pension plan.

For example, an employee who contributes £4,000 per year to a pension plan will still be £1,288 better off *every year* with a salary sacrifice arrangement (the same employee was £1,694 better off when all of the employer's national insurance saving was paid into the pension plan).

If you compare column 4 (the new salary sacrifice pension contribution) with column 2 (pension contribution before salary sacrifice) you will find that:

No matter how much basic-rate taxpayers contribute to a pension plan, they will still end up with 26% more money with a salary sacrifice arrangement... even if only half the employer's national insurance saving is paid into the pension plan.

TABLE 11
Sharing National Insurance Savings with the Employer:
Sample Pension Increases: Basic-Rate Taxpayers

Cash Contribution (1) £	Gross Contribution (2) £	Salary Sacrifice (3) £	New Contribution (4) £	Increase (5) £
500	625	735	786	161
750	938	1,103	1,179	242
1,000	1,250	1,470	1,571	321
1,250	1,563	1,838	1,965	403
1,500	1,875	2,206	2,358	483
1,750	2,188	2,574	2,751	564
2,000	2,500	2,941	3,144	644
2,250	2,813	3,309	3,537	725
2,500	3,125	3,676	3,930	805
2,750	3,438	4,044	4,323	886
3,000	3,750	4,412	4,716	966
3,500	4,375	5,147	5,502	1,127
4,000	5,000	5,882	6,288	1,288
4,500	5,625	6,618	7,074	1,449
5,000	6,250	7,353	7,860	1,610
5,500	6,875	8,088	8,646	1,771
6,000	7,500	8,824	9,432	1,932
6,500	8,125	9,559	10,218	2,093
7,000	8,750	10,294	11,004	2,254
7,500	9,375	11,029	11,790	2,415
8,000	10,000	11,765	12,576	2,576
8,500	10,625	12,500	13,363	2,738
9,000	11,250	13,235	14,149	2,899
9,500	11,875	13,971	14,935	3,060
10,000	12,500	14,706	15,721	3,221

Column descriptions:

1) **Cash Contribution.** A range of cash pension contributions, before the taxman's top up payment is added.

2) **Gross Contribution.** Found by dividing (1) by 0.8. This is the total gross pension contribution, ie with the taxman's top up payment added.

3) **Salary Sacrifice.** Found by dividing (1) by 0.68. The amount of salary you have to sacrifice while keeping your take-home pay constant.

4) **New Contribution.** This is simply column (3) plus 6.9%, representing **half** the employer's national insurance saving.

5) **Increase.** The increase in pension saving: (4) minus (2).

Higher Rate Taxpayers

Table 12 illustrates the annual benefit of a salary sacrifice arrangement for a whole range of different pension contribution amounts for *higher-rate taxpayers*.

The table is exactly the same as Table 9 in Chapter 24, except for columns 4 and 5. In column 4 only half the employer's national insurance saving is added to the employee's pension plan (6.9% instead of 13.8%).

Column 5 is the important one and shows how much better off a higher-rate taxpayer will be every year with a salary sacrifice arrangement, if only half the employer's national insurance saving is paid into his pension plan.

For example, an employee who contributes £6,000 per year to a pension plan will be £794 better off every year with a salary sacrifice arrangement (the same employee was £1,329 better off when all of the employer's national insurance saving was paid into the pension plan).

If you compare column 4 (the new salary sacrifice pension contribution) with column 2 (pension contribution before salary sacrifice) you will find that:

No matter how much higher-rate taxpayers contribute to a pension plan, they will still end up with 11% more money with a salary sacrifice arrangement... even if only half the employer's national insurance saving is paid into the pension plan.

TABLE 12
Sharing National Insurance Savings with the Employer:
Sample Pension Increases: Higher-Rate Taxpayers

Cash Contribution (1) £	Total Contribution (2) £	Salary Sacrifice (3) £	New Contribution (4) £	Increase (5) £
500	625	647	691	66
750	938	970	1,037	99
1,000	1,250	1,293	1,382	132
1,250	1,563	1,616	1,728	165
1,500	1,875	1,940	2,073	198
1,750	2,188	2,263	2,419	232
2,000	2,500	2,586	2,765	265
2,250	2,813	2,909	3,110	298
2,500	3,125	3,233	3,456	331
2,750	3,438	3,556	3,801	364
3,000	3,750	3,879	4,147	397
3,500	4,375	4,526	4,838	463
4,000	5,000	5,172	5,529	529
4,500	5,625	5,819	6,220	595
5,000	6,250	6,466	6,912	662
5,500	6,875	7,112	7,603	728
6,000	7,500	7,759	8,294	794
6,500	8,125	8,405	8,985	860
7,000	8,750	9,052	9,676	926
7,500	9,375	9,698	10,367	992
8,000	10,000	10,345	11,059	1,059
8,500	10,625	10,991	11,750	1,125
9,000	11,250	11,638	12,441	1,191
9,500	11,875	12,284	13,132	1,257
10,000	12,500	12,931	13,823	1,323
11,000	13,750	14,224	15,206	1,456
12,000	15,000	15,517	16,588	1,588
13,000	16,250	16,810	17,970	1,720
14,000	17,500	18,103	19,353	1,853
15,000	18,750	19,397	20,735	1,985
16,000	20,000	20,690	22,117	2,117
17,000	21,250	21,983	23,500	2,250
18,000	22,500	23,276	24,882	2,382
19,000	23,750	24,569	26,264	2,514
20,000	25,000	25,862	27,647	2,647

Employer Refuses to Share NI Savings

What happens if your employer refuses to share any of his national insurance savings? This is the worst-case scenario but cannot be ruled out.

If you are a basic-rate taxpayer a salary sacrifice pension is still worth having because your pension contributions will still be approximately 18% higher.

If you are a higher-rate taxpayer, however, a salary sacrifice pension will increase your pension contributions by a paltry 3%. Remember, higher-rate taxpayers only pay 2% national insurance on earnings over £41,865. So a salary sacrifice saves them very little unless some or all of the employer's much larger 13.8% national insurance bill is also added to the pension pot.

In summary, a salary sacrifice arrangement loses most of its attractiveness if you are a higher-rate taxpayer and your employer refuses to share his national insurance savings.

Summary

- Salary sacrifice requires your employer's approval.

- To convince your employer to introduce salary sacrifice you can use the following arguments:

    - Many big, reputable employers offer salary sacrifice
    - It is easy to implement
    - Mandatory pensions are currently being rolled out
    - It allows employers to provide FREE pay increases

- The national insurance savings can be shared with your employer. A basic-rate taxpayer could still end up with a 26% bigger pension pot. A higher-rate taxpayer could still end up with an 11% bigger pension pot.

- If your employer refuses to share any of his national insurance savings, a salary sacrifice arrangement is still worthwhile if you are a basic-rate taxpayer... but not very effective if you are a higher-rate taxpayer.

Chapter 26

Salary Sacrifice Drawbacks

With salary sacrifice pensions your gross salary is reduced, so anything that depends on your gross salary could be affected, including your:

- Employment benefits
- Borrowing ability
- Basic state pension
- State second pension (S2P)
- Maternity pay

Employment Benefits

If a salary sacrifice reduces your gross salary then this could *potentially* also reduce your:

- Future pay increases
- Overtime
- Life insurance cover provided by your employer
- Redundancy payments

I put the word 'potentially' in italics because many salary sacrifice arrangements address this issue by making sure all benefits are based on the employee's original salary – often referred to as the reference salary, notional salary or base salary.

So if you are currently earning £40,000 and your salary is reduced to £37,000, your employment benefits can be calculated on the basis that you are still earning £40,000.

One potential issue concerns refunds of employee pension contributions. If you currently belong to an occupational pension scheme and leave the company with less than two years' service, you may be entitled to a refund of the pension contributions you have made personally.

However, pension contributions made by your employer to an occupational pension scheme as part of a salary sacrifice arrangement are not employee contributions and may not be refunded.

Borrowing Ability

Any salary reduction could affect your ability to borrow money, for example to buy a house or for any other purpose.

One solution is for your employer to provide the lender with a letter of reference confirming your reference salary.

For example, many of the university salary sacrifice documents state that:

"You should quote your current annual salary on mortgage applications and your payslip will substantiate this figure as your annual salary. If The University Payroll Office receives requests for mortgage references from lenders they will quote your current salary i.e. before the reduction."

This potential issue can therefore be addressed. However, there is still a potential risk that some lenders will not accept your reference salary and use the lower post-sacrifice salary.

Basic State Pension

It is very unlikely that sacrificing some salary will affect your basic state pension entitlement. Your basic state pension is based on the number of years you have worked, not the amount of national insurance you have paid or the level of your salary.

Those on very low incomes have to be careful, however. If you earn less than the 'lower earnings limit' (LEL) in any year, that year will not be included in your contribution record when your basic state pension entitlement is calculated.

For the 2014/15 tax year the LEL is £5,772.

Other state benefits are also affected if your income falls below the LEL, including statutory sick pay, maternity pay, incapacity benefit and jobseekers' allowance.

The general consensus among pension experts is that you should not participate in a salary sacrifice arrangement if your income will fall below the LEL.

(Also, remember that your employer cannot let a salary sacrifice take you under the national minimum wage.)

For everyone else, as long as you have a full national insurance history, you will receive the full basic state pension when you reach the state pension age.

State Pension Basics

The state pension age will rise to 66 in 2020 for both men and women. By 2028 it will be 67.

The state pension age will be reviewed every five years. The government will take account of life expectancy projections and variations in life expectancy between rich and poor and between geographic regions.

In other words, the state pension age will probably continue to rise but only if everyone is living longer.

Although many regard the rise in the state pension age as unwelcome news, it comes as no surprise to those who understand how the state pension is funded. State pensions are not paid out of a big pot of money. Rather, the state pension system is really just a giant pyramid scheme: Those who are currently working pay the pensions of those who are retired.

The problem is that, with every year that passes, there are more people taking money out and fewer people putting money in!

At present there are four people of working age for every person over the state pension age. By 2050 there could be just two people of working age for every retired person.

Calculating Your Basic State Pension

How much basic state pension you receive currently depends on how many qualifying years you have built up. Qualifying years are years in which you pay, or are treated as having paid, national insurance.

To qualify for a full basic state pension you need 30 qualifying years.

For 2014/15 the maximum basic state pension for a single person is £5,881 per year and for married couples it is £9,407.

The basic state pension is indexed each year for those living in the UK, the European Union, the US and certain other countries.

However, more than half a million UK pensioners who have retired abroad do not enjoy any increases. These include retirees in Australia, Canada, Dubai, Hong Kong, India, New Zealand, Nigeria, Pakistan, Singapore, South Africa, Thailand, many Caribbean islands (except Barbados, Bermuda, and Jamaica), and Zimbabwe.

To obtain your very own state pension forecast go to:

www.gov.uk/state-pension-statement

State Second Pension (S2P)

Your state second pension is *currently* based on your gross salary, so sacrificing some salary may reduce your entitlement. I say 'may' because it all depends on how much you earn.

Even if your state second pension is reduced, in many cases the reduction will be tiny relative to the benefits you will enjoy from the salary sacrifice arrangement.

Furthermore, the way the state second pension is calculated is changing and these changes may limit any adverse impact from salary sacrifice arrangements in the future.

Calculating the State Second Pension

Most people don't know how their state second pension is calculated, so it's worth explaining briefly.

You build up your entitlement year by year. The amount added to your state pension account for the 2014/15 tax year is based on your earnings for the current year, using the following scale:

Earnings	Accrual
Below £5,772	£0
£5,772-£15,100	Flat rate £92 per year
£15,100-£40,040	10%
Above £40,040	£0

I'll explain how the table works shortly but first it is possible to make some general comments about how a salary sacrifice arrangement could affect your S2P entitlement:

- The first £0 figure in the table means that you accrue no S2P entitlement at all if your income is less than £5,772. So if a salary sacrifice takes your income below £5,772 you will lose your S2P entitlement for the current year.

  (This reinforces our recommendation earlier that those earning less than £5,772 should probably steer clear of salary sacrifice arrangements.)

- The second 0% figure means that you accrue no additional S2P entitlement on earnings over £40,040 (known as the upper accrual point). In other words, those earning above £40,040 get S2P based on £40,040. The £40,040 upper accrual point is fixed and does not increase with inflation, gradually losing value and reducing the earnings-related part of S2P.

This implies that:

If your earnings both before and after a salary sacrifice are over £40,040, your S2P entitlement will not be affected.

This means that Jane, our higher-rate taxpayer from earlier chapters, will not be affected. Her earnings both before and after the salary sacrifice are over £40,040.

- If you earn between £5,772 and £15,100 (known as the low earnings threshold) you are automatically treated as having earnings of £15,100. (The Government introduced this rule to help those on low incomes).

This means that:

If your earnings both before and after a salary sacrifice are between £5,772 and £15,100, your S2P entitlement will not be affected.

Those who *are* likely to be adversely affected by a salary sacrifice arrangement include the following:

- If your earnings both before and after a salary sacrifice are between £15,100 and £40,040. In this band your S2P accrual is based on your *actual earnings* so any reduction in your earnings will reduce your S2P accrual.

- A salary sacrifice causes your earnings to fall from one earnings band to another. For example, if your earnings fall from above £15,100 to below £15,100 you will lose your 10% accrual altogether for the current year. Similarly if your earnings fall from above £40,040 to below £40,040 you will lose some of your 10% accrual.

The next question is, how severely affected by salary sacrifice is your state second pension likely to be if you are one of the affected groups? This question is best answered with an example explaining how the state second pension is calculated:

Example – Before Salary Sacrifice

John earns £30,000 a year and has a working life of 49 years.

Using the earlier table, we calculate his S2P entitlement for the current year as follows:

Flat rate (earnings between £5,772 and £15,100) = £92
10% band: £30,000 less £15,100 = £14,900 x 10%/49 = £30
Total: £122

What this means is that, when John retires, he will receive a state second pension of £122 per year, based on his earnings for the 2014/15 tax year. This is just one year, of course, and there will be additional entitlement in respect of previous and future tax years.

The amount he will actually receive when he retires will be adjusted upwards with wage inflation but I have ignored this fact to keep the number crunching simple.

Example – After Salary Sacrifice

John sacrifices some salary and now earns £28,530 a year.

His S2P entitlement for the current year is as follows:

Flat rate (earnings between £5,772 and £15,100) = £92
10% band: £28,530 less £15,100 = £13,430 x 10%/49 = £27
Total: £119

What this means is that this year's salary sacrifice has reduced John's S2P entitlement by £3 per year. This is weighed against the benefits – a pension pot increase of £423.

State Pension – Future Changes

In January 2013 the Government announced a radical overhaul of the state pension system. The reforms will take effect from 6 April 2016 and will see the current basic state pension and second pension replaced with a flat-rate pension probably worth around £148 per week in today's money – roughly £7,700 per year.

In future, the state pension will be based solely on how many years of national insurance contributions or credits you have – the amount you earn will be irrelevant.

To qualify for the full state pension you will need 35 years of national insurance contributions or credits – five years more than at present. If you have less than 35 years you will get a proportion of the full state pension. For example, if you have 28 years of contributions you will get 80%.

To qualify for any state pension you will need a minimum level of contributions which will be set at between seven and 10 years. If you have less than this you will not receive any pension.

For those starting their working life after 5 April 2016, the new system is much simpler – you will simply get the flat–rate pension providing you have enough years of national insurance contributions.

If you are already working and have made national insurance contributions, your eventual state pension will be based on your previous national insurance record (the full value of your previous contributions will be preserved), and your future national insurance record after the switch to the single-tier state pension.

Maternity Pay

A salary sacrifice arrangement could reduce the amount of statutory maternity pay (SMP) to which you are entitled. Statutory maternity pay is based on your contractual earnings which count for national insurance contributions. So if your earnings have been reduced because you sacrificed some salary, the amount of statutory maternity pay you receive may also be reduced.

If a salary sacrifice takes your salary below the lower earnings limit (£5,772 in 2014/15), you will lose your statutory maternity pay entitlement altogether.

How is Statutory Maternity Pay Calculated?

Women are entitled to 52 weeks of maternity leave and 39 weeks of statutory maternity pay.

For the first six weeks you are entitled to receive 90% of your average gross weekly earnings, with no upper limit.

So, clearly, a salary sacrifice could reduce the amount of SMP you receive for the first six weeks.

For the remaining 33 weeks you are entitled to receive the *lesser* of:

- £138.18 per week
- 90% of your average earnings

All except the lowest paid will receive a flat amount of £138.18 per week for this 33-week period, so a salary sacrifice will probably have no effect on this part of your SMP entitlement.

Statutory Maternity Pay – Effect on the Employer

Employers are liable to pay statutory maternity pay but can get most of it refunded.

If the employer's total payments of class 1 national insurance are £45,000 or less he can recover 103% of the SMP paid.

The extra amount is to compensate him for the employer's national insurance payable on the SMP.

If the employer's total class 1 national insurance payments are more than £45,000 per year, the employer can recover 92% of the SMP paid.

Employer vs Employee

With salary sacrifice pensions the idea is that neither the employee nor the employer is worse off.

However, when it comes to the payment of non-cash benefits during maternity leave, it is possible the employer will be left out of pocket.

This is because employers have to continue providing any non-cash benefits that have been agreed under the contract of employment for up to 52 weeks (i.e. the full period of maternity leave).

Non-cash benefits include things like company cars and childcare vouchers.

There is some debate as to whether employer pension contributions have to be paid for the full 52 weeks of maternity leave but most accept that they have to be paid for the entire 39-week period of paid maternity leave.

The full amount has to be paid as though the woman was working normally and had taken no maternity leave at all.

Clearly, paying pension contributions could be more expensive to the employer than paying statutory maternity pay.

Maternity Allowance

Maternity allowance is paid to women who are employed but not entitled to SMP. Maternity allowance is based on your earnings, so a salary sacrifice arrangement may reduce your entitlement to maternity allowance.

Chapter 27

How to Implement a Salary Sacrifice Pension

It is important to point out that salary sacrifice must be a *contractual agreement*, not an informal arrangement between you and your employer.

In other words, you have to change your employment contract and this should to be done in writing.

It may be possible to change your contract of employment by using a simple agreement letter, signed by both you and your employer, and many pension companies provide sample documentation. This letter should be kept with your employment contract.

The new agreement must state what benefit is being received in exchange for the sacrificed salary.

Salary sacrifice can start at any time during the year but it's important that the potential future salary is given up before it is treated as received for tax and national insurance purposes. Your terms of employment must be changed *before* the salary sacrifice commences.

HMRC is not against salary sacrifice but could challenge the arrangement if it has not been set up correctly and the paperwork is not in order.

Year-end Pension Planning

The normal salary sacrifice rule is that the arrangement should last at least a year. However, with salary sacrifice *pensions* there is no longer a minimum period.

This may be of help to employees who want to do some year-end tax planning.

For example, in January 2015 you may realise that, if you receive your normal February and March pay cheques, you will pay the maximum child benefit charge (see Chapter 16).

With the agreement of your employer you may decide to reduce your salary for the two months (but not below the level of the national minimum wage), with matching pension contributions made by your employer.

Your salary could then be restored to its previous level at the start of the new tax year.

If there is opting in and out, each time there is a change there should be a legally enforceable variation to the employee's terms and conditions. It must be clear what the employee is entitled to in terms of cash pay and other benefits.

Getting HMRC Approval

HM Revenue & Customs does not have to be notified of salary sacrifice arrangements. However, after the arrangement is set up employers can ask their local tax offices to confirm that the correct tax treatment is being applied.

HMRC will probably want to see evidence that the employment contracts have been changed correctly, and payslips, before and after the sacrifice.

Details can also be sent to:

HMRC Clearances Team
Alexander House
21 Victoria Avenue
Southend-on-Sea
SS99 1BD

This gives the employer reassurance the arrangement has been implemented correctly.

Payslips and P60s

Strictly speaking, your new post-salary-sacrifice payslip should not show your old salary, with the sacrificed amount shown as a deduction.

However, HMRC's guidance notes state that if the employment contract has been changed correctly, the payslip is less important.

However, if there are issues surrounding the employment contract, the payslip may be used to determine whether the salary sacrifice is valid.

HMRC recognises that some payroll software can only store one value for the employee's salary. This could create problems when calculating overtime and other benefits based on the higher pre-sacrifice reference salary.

However, as long as the contract has been modified correctly, and makes it clear that the employee is entitled to a reduced salary and specified benefits, HMRC should not invalidate the salary sacrifice.

HMRC's guidance notes point out that non-taxable benefits-in-kind must not be carried forward to the P60.

Finally, I would strongly recommend speaking to a financial advisor who has experience of salary sacrifice pensions before diving in and setting one up yourself.

Chapter 28

Future and Recent Changes to National Insurance

Merging Income Tax & National Insurance

In his March 2012 Budget statement, the Chancellor of the Exchequer reiterated the Government's desire to merge income tax and national insurance:

"We are also pressing forward with our ambition to integrate the operation of income tax and national insurance I announced at last year's Budget – so we don't ask businesses to run two different payroll tax administrations."

The Government seems to accept that national insurance is just tax by another name. It would be far more honest to have a 32% basic rate of income tax, instead of 20% income tax plus 12% national insurance.

A merger of income tax and national insurance would possibly remove the need to set up salary sacrifice arrangements. Employees would, presumably, be able to obtain full tax relief by making their pension contributions personally.

However, don't expect this change to take place in the short term. According to HM Treasury:

"The detailed and extensive work the Government has done so far shows that this is a large and complex reform. The Government also understands that employers are adjusting to a large number of tax reforms that have already been set out.

Many are sceptical that such a radical reform of the tax system will take place at all, at least not before the next general election in May 2015. There would be winners but also losers and the coalition Government will probably not be able to afford creating more losers, following years of public spending cuts.

Writing in *The Times* after the 2011 Budget, former Chancellor of the Exchequer Nigel Lawson, who investigated such a reform in the 1980s, warned George Osborne that merging the two taxes is a "huge elephant trap":

"A merger of the two would, in practice, be very costly and (because there would be both winners and losers) highly unpopular, all to little advantage. So I say to George: Don't go there."

Whether such a significant change to the tax system is possible remains to be seen. However, there is little doubt that a Conservative Government would be committed to such a change on ideological grounds.

Such a change would make taxpayers more aware of the fact that they are actually paying 32% tax (plus an additional 13.8% tax paid by their employers), making it potentially less difficult to encourage support for a smaller role for Government in the economy and lower tax rates.

£2,000 National Insurance Allowance

Most businesses now receive an allowance of £2,000 per year to offset against their national insurance bills.

The national insurance allowance may reduce the attractiveness of salary sacrifice pensions to employees of the smallest companies – those employing just one or two people on low salaries and whose employer's national insurance bills are therefore no more than £2,000.

If the business doesn't have any national insurance to pay, thanks to the new allowance, a salary sacrifice will not produce an employer's national insurance saving that can be paid into the employees' pensions.

National Insurance for under 21s

From April 2015 employer's national insurance will be abolished for those under the age of 21 and earning no more than the upper earnings limit (£42,285 in 2015/16). Employer's national insurance will be payable as normal beyond this limit.

Part 7

Company Directors

Chapter 29

Introduction

Company directors, just like regular employees, can contribute up to 100% of their 'relevant UK earnings' to a pension but not more than £40,000 (the annual allowance).

Your relevant UK earnings will typically include your:

- Salary and any bonus
- Taxable benefits in kind

For example, a company director with a salary of £20,000 can make a cash contribution of up to £16,000. The taxman will top this up with £4,000 of basic-rate tax relief for a gross pension contribution of £20,000.

A company director with a salary of £50,000 can make a cash contribution of up to £32,000. The taxman will top this up with £8,000 of basic-rate tax relief for a gross pension contribution of £40,000. He can make an additional pension contribution of £10,000 gross if he has unused annual allowance from any of the previous three tax years.

(Of course, as we saw in Chapter 3, the director probably wouldn't want to make such a large contribution in practice because he would not receive higher-rate tax relief on the whole contribution.)

Company Pension Contributions

As a company owner you can also get your company (your employer) to make pension contributions on your behalf. Company pension contributions are always paid *gross* (there is no top up from the taxman) but the company will normally enjoy corporation tax relief on the payment.

For example, a small company making a pension contribution of £10,000 can claim corporation tax relief of £2,000 (£10,000 x 20% corporation tax relief).

Pension contributions made by employers are not restricted by the level of the employee's earnings. A company pension contribution can be bigger than the director's earnings. However, there are other restrictions on company pension contributions:

Firstly, total pension contributions by you and your company must not exceed the £40,000 annual allowance, although any unused allowance from the previous three tax years can be carried forward and used to cover contributions made by both you and the company.

Secondly, the company may be denied corporation tax relief on any pension contributions made on behalf of directors, if the taxman views them as 'excessive'. We'll return to this point later.

The critical question many company owners ask is: "Who should make the pension contributions: me or the company?"

Answering this question is the main focus of this part of the guide. However, before doing that it's important to explain how company owners often structure their pay to reduce income tax.

Chapter 30

Salary or Dividend?

Most company owners are both directors and shareholders. This means they can withdraw both salaries and dividends from their companies. Salaries are subject to income tax and national insurance; dividends are subject to income tax only.

Taking a big salary is generally not attractive because the national insurance cost is prohibitive. Up to 12% national insurance will have to be paid on a big chunk of the salary by the company owner personally and an extra 13.8% will usually have to be paid by the company.

But taking all the profits out as dividends is not the best solution for most small company owners either because this means subjecting all the company's profits to corporation tax (dividends are paid out of after-tax profits).

The optimal solution in most cases is to pay a small salary that is tax deductible in the company's hands and tax-free in the hands of the company owner.

Tax-free Salaries 2014/15

As a company owner trying to decide how much salary to pay yourself, there are two important thresholds where various taxes kick in:

- £7,956   12% and 13.8% national insurance
- £10,000   20% income tax

From a tax-saving perspective, it generally makes sense to pay yourself a salary equal to the national insurance threshold – £7,956 for 2014/15.

This will be tax free for the director because there is no income tax or national insurance. Furthermore, the salary will be a tax-deductible expense for the company resulting in a corporation tax saving of £1,591 (£7,956 x 20%).

So a small salary is even better than tax free, it produces a tax 'cashback' for the company!

It generally doesn't pay to take a salary of £10,000 instead of £7,956. There would be no income tax but there would be £527 of extra national insurance (£245 from the employee and £282 from the company). The corporation tax relief on the extra £2,044 salary and the £282 of employer's national insurance comes to £465 and therefore does NOT outweigh the £527 cost

$$(£2,044 + £282) \times 20\% = £465$$

In summary, the 'optimal' tax-free salary for a small company director in 2014/15 is £7,956 (although there may be other reasons why a higher salary is desirable).

Tax-free Dividends 2014/15

Company owners who are basic-rate taxpayers pay no income tax on their dividends. Higher-rate taxpayers pay income tax at an effective rate of 25% on their cash dividends.

How much do you have to earn to be a higher-rate taxpayer? With an income tax personal allowance of £10,000 and basic-rate band of £31,865, a higher rate-taxpayer is someone earning over £41,865.

So if you take a tax-free salary of £7,956 this leaves you scope to pay a tax-free *gross* dividend of up to £33,909 (£41,865 - £7,956).

Gross dividends include a 10% notional dividend tax credit. A gross dividend of £33,909 is thus equivalent to an actual cash dividend of £30,518 (£33,909 x 90%).

Total tax-free income: £38,474.

Bigger Dividends

If you want to take a bigger dividend in 2014/15, you can take additional cash dividends of up to £52,321 and the effective income tax rate on this extra income will be just 25%.

Anything more than this will take your gross taxable income over £100,000 – the point at which your income tax personal allowance begins to be withdrawn and your marginal tax rate increases dramatically.

Those with income over £150,000 will have to pay additional tax at the rate of 30.6% on their cash dividends.

There are many other factors to consider, of course, including the fact that any other taxable income you have in the same tax year must be taken into account when calculating your tax-free amounts. Your company must also have sufficient distributable profits before it can pay (or declare) any dividends.

Dividends – Formal Calculation

I mentioned above that higher-rate taxpayers pay income tax at 25% on their cash dividends. This is a useful shortcut calculation but most formal tax return computations actually work with *gross dividends*.

If you are a company director with dividend income you need to understand the formal dividend tax calculation if you want to maximise the higher-rate tax relief on your pension contributions.

To calculate your gross dividends you simply take your cash dividends and add on a 10% dividend tax credit. You do this by dividing your cash dividends by 0.9.

For example, if you pay yourself a cash dividend of £90, the gross dividend is £100 (£90/0.9) and the dividend tax credit is £10.

Gross dividends are taxed at 10% if you are a basic-rate taxpayer but you can subtract the 10% dividend tax credit, so the effective income tax rate is 0%.

Gross dividends are taxed at 32.5% if you are a higher-rate taxpayer but, once you subtract the 10% dividend tax credit, the effective income tax rate on gross dividends is 22.5%.

It's all unnecessarily complicated – a bit like climbing over a mountain instead of walking around the side – but UK tax law carries a lot of baggage like this from years gone by.

Finally, please note that I am not recommending that you structure your pay in the way described in this chapter. You should always speak to an accountant about your own optimal pay structure.

However, in the chapter that follows, where we look at pension contributions by directors and their companies, I am going to assume that directors structure their pay in this way.

Chapter 31

Pension Contributions: You or the Company?

Company Directors – Relevant UK Earnings

The pension contributions you make personally must not exceed your 'relevant UK earnings'. Salaries count as earnings; dividends do not.

For a small company director taking the optimal tax-free salary of £7,956, the maximum pension contribution that can be made is £7,956.

This is the maximum *gross* contribution. The director would personally invest £6,365 (£7,956 x 80%) and the taxman will top this up with £1,591 in basic-rate tax relief for a total gross contribution of £7,956.

Directors who want to make bigger pension contributions have two choices:

- Pay a bigger salary (ie more earnings)
- Get the company to make the contributions

In all situations, whether you want to make big pension contributions or small pension contributions, the key question is: What is more tax efficient, pension contributions made by you or your company?

Pension Contributions – You or the Company?

The short answer is this: If you want to make a relatively small pension contribution (no more than your small tax-free company salary) you should consider making the contribution personally. Additional contributions should be made by your company.

Why? Company directors who make contributions personally can enjoy up to 42.5% tax relief. For higher-rate taxpayers, company pension contributions, like most pension contributions, effectively provide 40% tax relief – still very attractive but not quite as attractive.

Company directors enjoy extra tax relief on the contributions they make personally thanks to an anomaly in the way gross dividends and gross pension contributions are calculated.

Let's now examine the issues with the help of some case studies.

Case Study 1
Company Director Makes Pension Contribution

Eva owns a small company called Cassidy Ltd. She takes a tax-free salary of £7,956 and a tax-free cash dividend of £30,518 for a total tax-free income of £38,474 (see previous chapter). She does not have any other taxable income.

If she makes a pension contribution with this level of income she will not be maximising her tax relief. She will not enjoy any higher-rate tax relief because she is a basic-rate taxpayer.

What she can do, if there are additional after-tax profits sitting in the company's bank account, is pay herself a bigger dividend. This would normally take Eva over the higher-rate threshold and be taxed but, coupled with a pension contribution, will be completely tax free.

Maximum Pension Contribution

Any pension contribution Eva makes personally cannot exceed her 'relevant UK earnings'. Salaries are earnings, dividends are not.

With a salary of £7,956, the maximum *gross* pension contribution she can make is £7,956.

This means Eva can personally invest £6,365 (£7,956 x 80%) and the taxman will add £1,591 in basic-rate tax relief for a total gross contribution of £7,956.

Optimal Additional Dividend

Eva extracts an extra cash dividend of £7,160. Note this is slightly more than the £6,365 she can personally invest in her pension. I'll explain why shortly.

In the absence of a pension contribution, this dividend would be fully taxed because she has already utilised her income tax personal allowance and basic-rate band for the current tax year.

A cash dividend of £7,160 equates to a gross dividend of £7,956 (£7,160 /0.9). As a higher-rate taxpayer now, Eva would normally pay 22.5% income tax on the additional dividend income, resulting in an income tax bill of £1,790.

Dividend and Pension Contribution

Eva personally invests £6,365 of the additional £7,160 cash dividend in her pension. The taxman will add £1,591 in basic-rate tax relief for a total gross pension contribution of £7,956.

What about Eva's higher-rate tax relief? As per normal, her basic-rate band will be increased by the amount of her gross pension contribution.

Eva's gross pension contribution was £7,956, so her basic-rate band will be increased by £7,956 and all of her additional £7,956 gross dividend will be tax free instead of taxed at 22.5%.

Eva's higher-rate tax relief is:

$$£7,956 \times 22.5\% = £1,790$$

The tax on her additional dividend income has been eliminated.

In total, Eva will enjoy £3,381 of tax relief (£1,591 basic-rate relief plus £1,790 higher-rate tax relief). This comes to 42.5% of her £7,956 gross pension contribution.

Most higher-rate taxpayers only enjoy 40% tax relief on their pension contributions, so this is an attractive outcome.

Why 42.5% Tax Relief?

This 'bonus' 2.5% tax relief comes about thanks to an anomaly in the way higher-rate tax relief is given to those with dividend income.

Eva's cash pension contribution of £6,365 results in a gross pension contribution of £7,956 (£6,365/0.8). This allows her to claim higher-rate tax relief on all of her £7,956 additional gross dividend.

But she has only had to contribute £7,072 of gross dividends into her pension (£6,365/0.9) to produce a £7,956 gross pension contribution.

Thus she is enjoying higher-rate tax relief on an additional £884 of gross dividends, which saves her an extra £194 in tax:

$$£884 \times 22.5\% = £199$$

The extra £199 tax saving is 2.5% of her gross pension contribution:

$$£199/£7,956 = 2.5\%$$

Other pension savers do not enjoy this bonus tax relief. You normally only enjoy higher-rate tax relief on the income you actually invest in your pension.

Do All Company Directors Enjoy 42.5% Tax Relief?

Eva gets higher-rate tax relief on the entire additional £7,956 gross dividend she took out of her company.

If she had only taken an additional £7,072 of gross dividends – just enough to make the maximum pension contribution – her higher-rate tax relief would be:

$$£7,072 \times 22.5\% = £1,591$$

(Remember higher-rate tax relief is always restricted to the amount of income you have subject to higher-rate tax.)

Combined with her £1,591 in basic-rate tax relief Eva would now enjoy only 40% tax relief, just like other taxpayers

$$£3,182/£7,956 = 40\%$$

The bottom line: As a company owner making pension contributions, you can enjoy 42.5% tax relief if you are a higher-rate taxpayer. Your gross dividends over the higher-rate threshold (£41,865 for 2014/15) must be at least as big as your gross pension contribution.

Final outcome: After making the pension contribution Eva has £7,956 in her pension pot and £39,269 of income, net of all taxes:

Original tax-free amounts	£38,474
Additional tax-free dividend	£7,160
Less: Cash pension contribution	£6,365
Total	£39,269

Case Study 2
Company Makes Pension Contribution

How would Eva fare if, instead of making the pension contribution personally, her company makes it?

The size of company contributions is not restricted by the level of an employee's earnings. However, for comparison purposes, we will assume that Cassidy Ltd also makes a £7,956 pension contribution (remember company pension contributions are always paid gross).

Eva will not obtain any tax relief personally but Cassidy Ltd will claim the amount as a corporation tax deduction. We will assume that Cassidy Ltd makes the contribution before the end of its accounting period, in other words before the company is subject to corporation tax on its profits.

To understand how a company pension contribution would affect Eva's financial position, we take the £7,160 of after-tax profits that she extracted as an additional dividend and add back the 20% corporation tax the company has to pay in the absence of a pension contribution:

Profits (£7,160/0.8)	£8,950
Less: Pension contribution	£7,956
Taxable profits	£994
Corporation tax @ 20%	£199
After-tax profits/cash dividend	£795
Income tax @ 25%	£199
After-tax dividend	£596

Eva's total after-tax income now consists of her initial tax-free dividend and salary and her additional after-tax dividend:

$$£38,474 + £596 = £39,070$$

As before, Eva has £7,956 sitting in her pension pot but her after-tax disposable income has fallen by £199 from £39,269 to £39,070.

Remember £199? That's the 2.5% bonus tax relief Eva enjoys when she makes the pension contribution personally.

In summary, Eva is better off making the pension contribution personally. Company pension contributions effectively produce 40% tax relief compared with 42.5% when the director makes them personally.

40% Tax Relief – Company Pension Contribution

Tax relief at 40% may be less than 42.5% but is not to be sneered at, especially by company directors like Eva who have low salaries and can therefore only make limited pension contributions personally.

Company pension contributions are an excellent way to extract additional money from your company in a tax-efficient manner.

But why do we say that company pension contributions produce 40% tax relief? In the above example Cassidy Ltd was only enjoying 20% corporation tax relief on the pension contribution it made for Eva.

When it comes to company owners you have to look at the complete picture: the cost to both the director and the company of getting additional money out of the company.

If, instead of getting her company to make a tax-deductible pension contribution of £7,956, Eva had taken the income as a dividend, both she and her company would pay the following taxes:

Pre-tax profits	£7,956
Corporation tax @ 20%	£1,591
After-tax profits/cash dividend	£6,365
Income tax @ 25%	£1,591
After-tax dividend	£4,774

The total extra tax would be £3,182 which is 40% of £7,956.

In summary, getting your company to make pension contributions could be a tax-efficient way to extract profits for your personal benefit. Total tax relief comes to 40%.

Additional Pension Contributions

Eva is better off making her pension contributions personally if she is happy to restrict them to the amount of her £7,956 tax-free salary.

If Eva wants to make an additional pension contribution in excess of her salary, she has two choices:

- Pay herself more salary (more earnings) and make the contribution personally

- Get the company to make the additional contribution

Paying more salary could be a bad idea from a tax-saving perspective because the additional salary will attract 12% employee's national insurance and 13.8% employer's national insurance. None of this national insurance can be avoided because pension contributions made by individuals only attract income tax relief.

Case Study 3
Additional Salary vs Company Contribution

Let's assume Eva wants to make an additional pension contribution of £10,000.

We'll assume she has taken the salary and dividends mentioned above and has made a pension contribution of £7,956 personally.

We'll also assume the company has pre-tax profits of £100,000. She now has two choices: pay an extra £10,000 of salary or get her company to make a £10,000 pension contribution.

Company's Position

	Company Makes Pension Contribution	Director Takes Additional Salary
	£	£
Pre-tax profits	100,000	100,000
Less:		
Salary	7,956	17,956
Employer's NI (13.8% over £7,956)	0	1,380
Company pension contribution	10,000	0
Net profits	82,044	80,664
Corporation tax @ 20%	16,409	16,133
After-tax profits	65,635	64,531
Less cash dividends:		
Initial dividend*	30,518	30,518
Additional dividend**	7,160	7,160
Remaining after-tax profits	**27,957**	**26,853**

* Initial tax-free divided to utilise the basic-rate band
** Additional dividend to fund director's own pension contribution

By getting the company to make the £10,000 pension contribution, instead of taking £10,000 of additional salary, the company is left with £1,104 more in its bank account.

This difference is down to the fact that employer's national insurance has to be paid on the additional salary but not on the company pension contribution.

The additional national insurance is £1,380 but this cost is a tax-deductible cost for the company so the net cost is £1,104 (£1,380 less 20% corporation tax relief).

Eva's personal position is compared below. The left-hand column shows how Eva fares when the company makes the £10,000 additional pension contribution.

This column contains all the numbers discussed in previous sections. Eva's after-tax income is completely unaffected by the company pension contribution.

The only difference is at the very bottom where her pension pot now has an extra £10,000 sitting in it.

The right-hand column shows how Eva fares with an additional £10,000 of salary and making the pension contribution personally.

She ends up £791 better off with a company pension contribution.

This difference is mainly down to the fact that she would have to pay £1,200 national insurance on the extra salary. She has to pay £1,591 income tax but this is more than offset by £2,000 of basic-rate tax relief on the additional pension contribution. (£2,044 of the extra salary is tax free because she still has some of her income tax personal allowance remaining.)

In total, Eva and her company are better off to the tune of almost £2,000 by getting the company to make the additional pension contribution.

The savings can be explained by the additional national insurance cost of paying salaries.

In summary, the most tax-efficient strategy for many company directors is to make a relatively small pension contribution personally (no more than the tax-free company salary).

Thereafter, company pension contributions may be an excellent way to extract additional money from the company in a tax-efficient manner. They are normally a tax-deductible expense and there is no income tax or national insurance payable on the amount.

Director's Position

	Company Makes Pension Contribution £	Director Takes Additional Salary £
Salary	7,956	17,956
Less:		
Employee's NI (salary - £7,956 x 12%)	0	1,200
Income tax (salary - £10,000 x 20%)	0	1,591
After-tax salary	**7,956**	**15,165**
Dividend Income		
Initial dividend	30,518	30,518
Additional dividend	7,160	7,160
Total cash dividends	37,678	37,678
Gross dividends (cash dividends/0.9)	41,865	41,865
Tax-free within basic-rate band:		
(£41,865 – salary)	33,909	23,909
Taxable gross dividend	7,956	17,956
Income tax @ 22.5%	1,790	4,040
Higher-rate tax relief:		
Gross pension contribution x 22.5%	1,790	4,040
After-tax cash dividends	**37,678**	**37,678**
Cash Pension Contributions		
Gross pension contributions x 0.8	6,365	14,365
Net Income	**39,269**	**38,478**
Pension Pot		
Cash pension contributions	6,365	14,365
Basic-rate relief	1,591	3,591
Company pension contributions	10,000	0
Total	17,956	17,956

Restrictions on Company Pension Contributions

The important thing to note about company pension contributions is you do not need a dedicated company pension scheme to make them.

Most providers of personal pensions, like SIPPs, have special forms that allow your company to pay directly into them.

How much can the company contribute? The company's contributions are not limited to your salary earnings, but it is important to remember the annual allowance: the maximum total gross pension contributions that can be made by both you and your company may be limited to £40,000.

Furthermore, there is a danger that HM Revenue & Customs will deny corporation tax relief for 'excessive' pension contributions. Company pension contributions will only be a tax deductible expense if they are incurred wholly and exclusively for the purposes of the trade.

When determining whether company pension contributions qualify for corporation tax relief, HMRC will look at the total remuneration package of the director/shareholder. The total package (including salary, pension contributions and other benefits in kind) must not be excessive relative to the work the individual carries out and his or her responsibilities.

Relevant factors may include:

- The number of hours you work, your experience and your level of responsibility in the company.

- The pay of other similar employees in your company and other companies.

- The pay required to recruit someone to take over your duties.

- The company's financial performance.

Extra care may be necessary in the event of a large one-off company pension contribution.

It may be sensible to document the commercial justification (e.g. strong recent financial performance of the company) in the minutes of a directors' board meeting and hold a shareholders' meeting to approve the contribution.

Although the risk that your company will be denied corporation tax relief may be small, it is important to stress that, when it comes to company pension contributions, unlike many contributions made by individuals, there is no cast-iron guarantee that the company will enjoy tax relief.

That's why I would recommend speaking to a tax advisor before your company starts making significant contributions.

National Insurance Allowance

In this chapter we have ignored the effect of the new national insurance allowance. Most businesses now receive an allowance of £2,000 per year to offset against their national insurance bills.

The assumption is that the allowance is used up paying salaries to other employees who are not the directors/shareholders.

However, in very small companies where the directors are the only salary earners, it is now possible for them to receive a higher salary with no employer's national insurance payable.

For example, where there is only one director in receipt of a salary, it is possible for the director to receive a salary of up to £22,449 with no employer's national insurance payable.

$$(£22,449 - £7,956) \times 13.8\% = £2,000$$

Such a salary would continue to be subject to employee's national insurance at 12% in the normal way.

Part 8

The Self Employed & Property Investors

Chapter 32

Pension Planning for the Self Employed

The number of self-employed business owners saving for retirement has fallen dramatically in recent years.

According to HMRC figures, back in 2002/3 there were 1.2 million self-employed individuals making personal pension contributions. By 2009/10 the number had almost halved to 660,000. The average gross contribution was just £3,030 per year.

When HMRC uses the term 'self employed' they are referring specifically to owners of unincorporated businesses, ie sole traders and partnerships. Most company owners are classified as employees (see Part 7 for more on company owners).

Most of the chapters in this guide are relevant for self-employed individuals. However, there are a few additional points that need to be made.

In particular, to maximise the tax relief on your pension contributions it is important to know how much taxable income you have. Most regular employees know how much taxable income they have: all they have to do is look at their payslips!

Many company owners also know how much taxable income they earn *personally*. The *company's* profits may fluctuate from year to year but many directors know how much salary or dividend income they are going to withdraw.

The taxable income of self-employed business owners is often much harder to predict. Taxable income for these individuals is normally the pre-tax profits of the business and there could be significant swings from year to year.

For example, a big order before the end of the tax year could increase taxable profits significantly. Several months of poor trading conditions could see profits fall sharply or even produce a loss for the year.

Sometimes it's not just the sales of the business that will result in big changes to taxable income. The business owner may deliberately drive down taxable profits, for example by making investments in tax-deductible equipment (e.g. vans or computers).

So what has all this got to do with maximising tax relief on pension contributions?

Well for starters, in Chapter 2 we pointed out that to enjoy any tax relief on your pension contributions you must have 'relevant UK earnings'. If your business makes a loss you won't have any earnings and the maximum pension contribution you can make is £3,600 (the 'universal pension contribution' that everyone under age 75 can make).

In Chapter 3 we pointed out that to maximise your higher-rate tax relief, your gross pension contributions should not exceed the amount of income you have over the higher-rate threshold (£41,865 in 2014/15). In other words, someone with taxable income of £50,000, who wants to maximise their higher-rate tax relief, should make a gross pension contribution of no more than £8,135 (£50,000 – £41,865).

A sole trader with bumper profits of £85,000 may want to make a big catch-up pension contribution of, say, £40,000 but reduce it to, say, £3,000 if his taxable profits fall back to £45,000.

In Chapter 14 we discussed the pros and cons of postponing pension contributions if you are a temporary basic-rate taxpayer. For example, during tough economic times (or if the business has a lot of tax-deductible expenditure for the year) the business owner may become a basic-rate taxpayer and decide to postpone making pension contributions until he becomes a higher-rate taxpayer in a future tax year.

Finally, in Chapter 16 we explained why self-employed business owners may wish to make bigger than normal pension contributions during tax years in which their profits are £50,000 to £60,000, in order to avoid the new child benefit tax charge.

Calculating Pre-tax Profits

Although many sole traders may want to vary the amount they contribute to a pension each year in order to maximise their tax relief, the problem for some is they don't know how much profit the business is making!

They may only have this information after they draw up their accounts for the year. This may happen many months after the tax year has ended – in other words, when it is too late to make pension contributions (remember you cannot make backdated pension contributions).

Example
Elliott is a sole trader with a 31 March year end.

On 5 April 2015 (the final day of the 2014/15 tax year) he makes a net cash pension contribution of £6,000. The taxman adds £1,500 of basic-rate tax relief for a gross pension contribution of £7,500. Elliott expects to have pre-tax profits of £50,000 for 2014/15 and therefore expects to receive £1,500 of higher-rate tax relief (£7,500 x 20%).

Elliott's accountant finishes drawing up the accounts for the business in July 2015 and, after taking account of all of his tax-deductible expenditure, calculates that Elliott has pre-tax profits of £45,000.

This means Elliott will only enjoy higher-rate tax relief on £3,135 of his gross pension contribution (£45,000 - £41,865), saving him just £627 in higher-rate tax (£3,135 x 20%). If Elliott had known that his profits would turn out to be £5,000 lower he may have held onto some of his cash and made a bigger pension contribution in a future tax year when his income was higher.

The problem for Elliott is he had just five days from the end of his business accounting period to the end of the tax year to calculate his pre-tax profits and make a pension contribution that produced the maximum amount of higher-rate tax relief.

Most business owners would find this difficult if not impossible to do and very few accountants would be prepared to work to such a tight deadline.

Some business owners have a 5 April year end and therefore no time at all to accurately calculate their pre-tax profits.

Uncertainty about the level of pre-tax profits is less of a problem for business owners who are confident their pre-tax profits will exceed the higher-rate threshold by a big margin, especially if their pension contributions are quite modest (for example, someone who reckons pre-tax profits will be £80,000 and wants to make a £5,000 pension contribution).

However, it could be a problem even for high earners if they want to make big catch-up pension contributions and want higher-rate tax relief on the lot (for example, someone who expects to make pre-tax profits of £85,000 and wants to make a £40,000 pension contribution).

Changing the Accounting Year End

One option is to change your accounting year end to a date other than the tax year.

For example, let's say the business year end is 30 April 2014. This year end falls into the 2014/15 tax year which means the business owner would have from 30 April 2014 until the end of the tax year on 5 April 2015 to draw up accounts and decide what level of pension contribution to make.

Changing your accounting date has other tax benefits and drawbacks. For more information see the Taxcafe guide, *Small Business Tax Saving Tactics*.

Chapter 33

Pension Planning for Property Investors

When I started out writing this guide, I planned to conduct a comprehensive study comparing pensions and buy-to-let property. However, I quickly abandoned this idea for two reasons.

Firstly, a pension is not an asset. It is simply a 'wrapper' that protects the underlying assets from tax. Those assets are normally shares but also bonds and perhaps commodities like gold or even commercial property (but not residential property which is prohibited).

So any comparison of pensions and buy-to-let ultimately boils down to a comparison of stock market investing and residential property investing. Plenty of academics have conducted studies to see which asset class performs best, but the results are sensitive to the time period under consideration and, critically, whether you include rents and dividends in the analysis.

The second reason why I decided not to spend time comparing pensions and buy-to-let property is that many property investors would simply not countenance investing in anything else. "Nothing beats bricks and mortar," goes the popular mantra.

I've lost count of the number of times I've heard the phrase "my properties are my pension".

So what I've decided to do in this chapter is explore how a pension can be used to *complement* an investment in buy-to-let property and give it extra fire power.

Healthy Rental Profits = Unhealthy Tax Bill

Many landlords are currently enjoying healthy rental profits thanks to strong demand for rented accommodation and relatively low interest rates on buy-to-let mortgages.

The bad news is that rental profits are taxed much more heavily than capital gains. Rental profits are added to your other income and typically taxed at 20% or 40%.

Looked at purely from a tax-saving perspective, income from property is a lot less attractive than income from other investments such as shares with high dividend yields or bonds. Dividends and interest income are completely tax free if you put your money in an ISA or pension. Rental income from residential property generally cannot be sheltered from the taxman.

Example
Samantha is a higher-rate taxpayer and earns rental profits of £10,000 during the tax year. Her total tax bill is £4,000 (£10,000 x 40%).

Miriam is a higher-rate taxpayer and earns dividends of £10,000 from shares held inside a pension. Her dividend income is completely tax free.

In summary, Miriam enjoys £4,000 more income than Samantha, possibly every year.

Knowing that Miriam's after-tax income is higher may not be of any use to Samantha because she already owns buy-to-let property. It could be expensive to sell up and put the money into a pension, even if she wanted to. If you already own rental property, a more important question is: What can be done to lower the taxable rental profits?

The answer depends on what you intend to do with your rental profits. Rental profits can be put to use in a number of different ways and some are more tax efficient than others:

Option #1 Spend the Money!

Many property investors rely on their rental profits to supplement their other income and pay the household bills. However, if you regard your properties as your pension, as many property investors do, this is arguably the least prudent thing you can do.

Option #2 Build an Emergency Cash Reserve

Unlike most other investments, rental properties can make big demands on your wallet from time to time. Instead of being a source of income they can become a source of additional costs.

I know this because I am a property investor myself. Recently I forked out £2,500 for a new boiler in one of my properties and paid several thousand pounds to repair water damage in another.

An emergency cash reserve will protect against unforeseen expenses or properties lying empty for several months while mortgage interest costs are racked up.

Option #3 Reduce Mortgages

This may be a good way to spend your rental profits if you are the type of investor who dislikes debt. Paying down buy-to-let mortgages is certainly worth considering if you think your properties may fall in value or mortgage interest rates will rise.

However, you should consider reducing any mortgage on your own home first. This interest is generally not tax deductible, so pound for pound it is more expensive than interest on a buy-to-let mortgage, which is generally tax deductible.

For example, let's say paying off some of your buy-to-let mortgage reduces your interest bill by £100 per year. This will give you £100 more rental profit but you will be left with just £60 after tax if you are a higher-rate taxpayer.

By contrast, let's say paying off the same amount of any mortgage on your home also reduces your interest bill by £100 per year. This will leave you with £100 more disposable income. Clearly, paying off interest on a home loan is more tax efficient (unless the interest rate on the buy-to-let mortgage is significantly higher).

Option #4 Buy More Rental Property

You may wish to save up your rental profits to buy new properties. Samantha may have to wait up to five years to save up enough after-tax rental profit to afford a £30,000 deposit on a new property costing £150,000:

£6,000 after-tax rental income x 5 years = £30,000

It remains an option but a clumsy one.

If you use your rental profits for options 1 to 4, there is very little you can do to reduce the immediate income tax bill on your rental profits. If you spend your rental profits, build an emergency cash reserve, reduce your mortgages or buy more rental property you will have to do so using after-tax profits.

However, there are two other strategies that may either reduce or completely eliminate the income tax on your rental profits:

Option #5 Upgrade Properties

If you spend money on your existing properties, the expense is normally treated as either a repair or an improvement.

Repairs are immediately tax deductible and will save you income tax. Obvious examples of repairs are things that require urgent attention: broken windows, faulty boilers, etc. This type of repair is normally dealt with by the landlord immediately so discretionary tax planning doesn't come into the picture.

Improvements are not so good from a tax-saving perspective because tax relief is only provided when the property is sold and will only save you up to 28% capital gains tax. Improvements are generally new features that were not present in the property before and therefore increase its value: extensions, attic conversions, etc.

Between these two extremes is what I call 'hybrid repairs': they give you full income tax relief AND may increase the value of your property and/or increase its rental potential.

Examples include: New kitchens, new bathrooms, double glazing, re-wiring and most decorating costs. Many property investors think of these items as improvements but they are in fact fully tax-deductible repairs... provided you follow the rules. To be treated as repairs it is important that you replace old items with new items and do not add something new that was not present before.

For example, replacing a tatty old kitchen is a tax-deductible repair. If you add extra kitchen units or sockets, these additional items will be improvements. Replacing a pea-green bathroom is a tax-deductible repair. Installing a shower or downstairs toilet where there wasn't one before is an improvement.

When replacing old items it is also important that you do not substantially upgrade the quality – that would be an improvement. However, it IS acceptable to install items that are of superior quality when they are simply the nearest modern equivalent, for example, replacing old single glazing with double glazing.

Although this is a tax-efficient way to spend your rental profits there is no guarantee that these hybrid repairs will always increase the value of your property or your rental income (or enough to make them worthwhile). There's also a limit to the amount of hybrid repairs you can carry out, so they are not a permanent solution to your income tax problem.

Option #6 Make Pension Contributions

If Samantha, the property investor, doesn't want to spend any money on repairs one thing she can do to completely offset the income tax payable on her £10,000 of rental profits is make a pension contribution.

If Samantha invests £8,000 of her rental profits the taxman will add £2,000 of basic-rate tax relief directly to her pension pot resulting in a gross pension contribution of £10,000.

She will also enjoy higher-rate tax relief. Her basic-rate band will be extended by £10,000 (her gross pension contribution) which means her £10,000 rental profit will only be taxed at 20% instead of 40%.

The total tax bill is £2,000 and is covered by the £2,000 of rental profit she did not invest in her pension. All in all she has £10,000 sitting in her pension, compared with the £6,000 she had sitting in her bank account previously.

She can do this every year and build a nice additional nest egg. After 10 years she could have around £150,000 sitting in her pension pot (assuming the money grows by 7% per year tax free).

If she hadn't made a conscientious effort to reinvest her rental profits they probably would have been either frittered away or left earning a very low rate of interest in her bank account.

Landlord Pension Contributions – Other Issues

Before making pension contributions to offset the income tax payable on your rental income you should remember the following:

- **Do you have earnings?** Everyone under 75 can contribute up to £3,600 per year to a pension. If you want to contribute more than this you must have 'earnings'. Salaries and business profits are earnings; rental profits generally are not. If you want to make big pension contributions to reduce the income tax on your rental income, you must have earnings from other sources.

- **Do you have enough income taxed at 40%?** For Samantha to enjoy higher-rate tax relief on her entire £10,000 pension contribution she must have at least £10,000 of income taxed at 40%. In other words, her total taxable income (including her rental profits) must be at least £51,865 in 2014/15.

- **How much rental profit do you have?** To accurately offset the income tax payable on your rental profits you may wish to calculate your rental profits before 5 April each year. Leave yourself enough time to do this.

- **Are you happy to invest in other assets?** Pension savings cannot be used to invest in bricks and mortar residential property. Most people invest in shares and bonds, although commercial property is permissible, including commercial property funds.

Part 9

Family Pension Planning

Chapter 34

Couples: Who Should Make the Pension Contributions?

People without earnings (i.e. who don't work) can make a pension contribution of £2,880 per year. The taxman will add £720 of basic-rate tax relief, resulting in a gross pension contribution of £3,600.

Is this worth doing?

Some people think it is because, although there will only be basic-rate tax relief, the ultimate pension income may end up being completely tax free, covered by the individual's income tax personal allowance.

The broader question that needs answering is this:

Under what circumstances should you transfer money to a spouse or partner to make pension contributions?

We can answer this question with the aid of a case study.

Case Study

Rory is a higher-rate taxpayer and his wife Claire is either a basic-rate taxpayer or doesn't work at all (whichever you prefer). Rory contributes to a pension, Claire doesn't. The couple want to make additional pension contributions and are trying to decide *who* should make them.

Rory will enjoy higher-rate tax relief on his extra pension contributions BUT he expects to ultimately pay 20% income tax on his pension income. Claire will only enjoy basic-rate tax relief on her pension contributions BUT she hope to pay 0% tax on her pension income (being fully covered by her personal allowance).

Let's assume the couple want to save an additional £2,880 annually. If Claire makes the contributions, the taxman will add £720 of basic-rate tax relief, producing a gross pension contribution of £3,600.

Rory can make a net cash contribution of £3,840. The taxman will add £960 of basic-rate relief, resulting in a gross contribution of £4,800. Rory will also receive £960 of higher-rate tax relief (£4,800 x 20%), so the net cost to him is also £2,880 (£3,840 - £960).

Every year Rory has an extra £4,800 going into his pension, whereas Claire only has £3,600.

If the money grows by 7% per year then after 20 years Rory's additional contributions will have grown to £210,553, whereas Claire will have £157,915.

In summary, Rory ends up with 33% more money than Claire... but this is no real surprise (see Chapter 14).

Withdrawing Income

Let's say they pass the minimum retirement age and decide to withdraw money from their pensions. They both take a 25% tax-free lump sum and invest the money in ISAs to produce tax-free retirement income (in practice this exercise may take several tax years to complete).

The remaining 75% is used to provide taxable pension income. We'll assume that both the ISA savings and pension savings produce income of 7% per year.

(See Chapter 12 where I used a similar number. In practice, Claire may wish to withdraw a smaller pension income because, as a woman, she has a longer life expectancy. I am ignoring this fact to keep things simple and because it does not affect the final outcome.)

Their after-tax incomes are summarised in Table 13. Total after-tax income includes the tax-free ISA income and the after-tax pension income.

Table 13
Couples Pension Planning
Who Should Make Contributions?

	Higher-rate relief on contributions	Basic-rate relief on contributions
	£	£
Total pension pot	210,553	157,915
25% Lump sum for ISA	52,638	39,479
ISA income - 7%	3,685	2,764
Balance in pension pot	157,915	118,436
Pre-tax income - 7%	11,054	8,291
Total after-tax income:		
After-tax @ 0%	14,739	11,055
After-tax @ 20%	12,528	9,397
After-tax @ 40%	10,317	7,739

When Rory Should Make the Contributions

If Rory pays 20% income tax when he retires (remember he has other pension savings) he will end up with £12,528. If Claire pays 0% income tax (because she has no other pension savings and her pension income is covered by her personal allowance) she will end up with £11,055. Rory receives 13% more income.

So the first conclusion is this: Rory should keep on making the pension contributions, even if Claire's pension income will be tax free.

It's even more important that Rory makes the contributions if there is any likelihood that Claire will acquire another source of income (e.g. from rental properties, inherited assets, a business or job etc). If Claire ends up being taxed at 20% on her pension income she may end up with £9,397 to Rory's £12,528. Rory receives 33% more income in this scenario.

When Claire Should Make the Contributions

But what if Rory, like Claire, does not receive higher-rate tax relief on these additional pension contributions, only basic-rate tax relief? This would be the case if his existing pension contributions are already equal to the amount of income he has subject to higher-rate tax (see Chapter 3 for an explanation).

In this case Rory would end up with £9,397 to Claire's £11,055. Claire receives 18% more income in this scenario.

So the second conclusion is this: Claire should make the additional contributions if Rory cannot obtain any additional higher-rate tax relief and she expects to pay no tax on her pension income. It's a second-best outcome but may be the best route for some couples.

If Rory expects to be a higher-rate taxpayer when he retires (perhaps because he has a lot of other pension savings or other assets that produce taxable income) he could end up with £10,317 to Claire's £11,055. Claire receives 7% more income in this scenario and should therefore consider making the contributions.

In most cases Claire only ends up better off than Rory if she pays 0% tax on her pension income. However, if she works she will eventually receive a taxable state pension which will probably use up most of her personal allowance which means she will pay 20% tax on most of her other pension income.

Even if Claire has never worked she may receive some state pension. For example, she will build up state pension entitlement while she has children under 12 and qualifies for child benefit.

In these cases Claire may only be able to pay 0% tax on all her pension income if all her pension savings are withdrawn before she reaches state pension age. This will only be possible if she has a relatively small pension pot.

Less Common Scenarios

There are other permutations, including Rory paying 0% tax when he retires (the best-case scenario of all) and Claire paying 40% tax when she retires (the worst-case scenario of all) but these outcomes are less likely and will not be discussed further.

Avoiding the Child Benefit Charge

If Claire receives child benefit and Rory's taxable income is in the £50,000-£60,000 bracket, he should probably be the one making all the pension contributions.

This will allow him to reduce or avoid the child benefit tax charge and enjoy over 50% tax relief on his pension contributions (see Chapter 16).

Family Tax Planning and Other Issues

Finally, it's worth pointing out that Claire may have *non-tax* reasons for making pension contributions, for example if she feels this gives her greater financial security.

On this note it should be pointed out that there are other things the couple can do to make use of Claire's tax-free personal allowance before she receives any state pension. For example, rental properties and other assets could be placed in her name, as could money the couple may eventually inherit.

Chapter 35

Pensions for Children and Grandchildren

"When I was a boy of 14, my father was so ignorant I could hardly stand to have the old man around. But when I got to be 21, I was astonished at how much the old man had learned in seven years."
Mark Twain

Everyone under the age of 75 can make a pension contribution of £3,600 per year and receive basic-rate tax relief (which reduces the net cost to £2,880).

This means minor children can make pension contributions or, as is more likely in practice, their parents or grandparents can contribute on their behalf.

Many pension providers have special pension plans for minors, like the Junior SIPP from Hargreaves Lansdown. According to HM Revenue and Customs, around 60,000 children under 18 years of age are making use of this tax break.

Making pension contributions on behalf of a minor child could be a wonderful way to leave an asset of lasting value that cannot be frittered away, at least not until the child is a responsible pensioner!

These contributions have the added bonus of usually being exempt from inheritance tax, being covered by either the £3,000 annual inheritance tax exemption or the regular gifts out of income exemption.

Thanks to the magic of compound growth, a pension contribution made on behalf of a minor child could grow into a significant nest egg. For example, let's say you make 18 annual contributions of £2,880 starting in the year a child is born. Each contribution will be topped up with £720 of basic-rate tax relief (even though the child doesn't pay any income tax), producing a gross pension contribution of £3,600 per year.

If we assume that the investments in the pension grow by 7% per year, just before the child's 18th birthday, when the last contribution is made, the pension pot will be worth £122,397. However, that's not the end of the story. The money will continue to compound tax free until the child is at least 59 (the possible minimum retirement age). Just before the 59th birthday the money will have grown to £1.96 million.

Of course these figures aren't adjusted for inflation. If some inflation adjustments are made you still end up with a pension pot worth over £350,000 in today's money, which is still a tidy sum!

Junior ISAs

In 2011 a new savings vehicle, the Junior ISA, was introduced. Just like normal ISAs, money grows tax free but there is no upfront tax relief, as there is with pension contributions.

The annual investment limit is £4,000 from July 2014.

Unlike regular ISAs, money cannot be withdrawn until the child reaches age 18. From that date the junior ISA becomes an adult ISA and the child can do what he or she likes with the money.

Junior SIPP vs Junior ISA

There's no doubt that most children or grandchildren would prefer you to contribute to a junior ISA instead of a junior SIPP. They will face big financial commitments between the age of 18 and 59, e.g. university fees, buying a home or raising children of their own.

However, there is also the risk that the child will fritter away all of that carefully saved up money, if they can access it at the tender age of 18.

Personally I prefer the pension route for the simple reason that your children or grandchildren are going to have to save for retirement anyway. In other words, they can never lose out with a pension but they can lose out with a junior ISA that is not spent wisely.

They'll thank you for it... one day!

Lightning Source UK Ltd.
Milton Keynes UK
UKOW04f0013170514

231763UK00001B/2/P